The Art of J. L. Shively

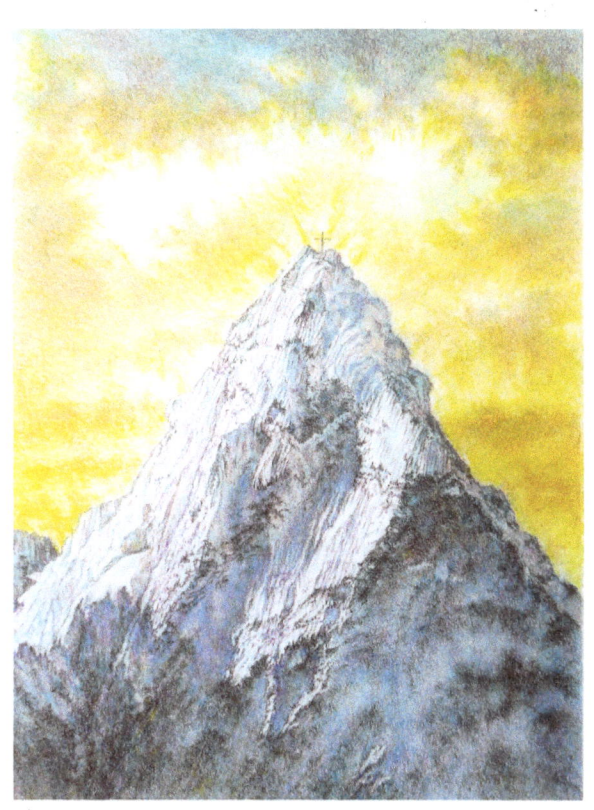

Art with a Message

ISBN 979-8-218-25257-1

Copyright 2023 by
J.L. Shively

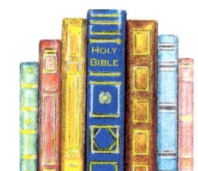

"And you shall know the truth, and the truth shall make you free"
John 8:32

All scriptures taken from the King James Version, adapted into contemporary English when appropriate. All rights reserved. No part of this book may be photocopied, stored electronically, duplicated or reproduced in any other format.

*This book
is dedicated
to the
One True God of Israel
and His Son
The Messiah Jesus,
whose words are
the inspiration
for the artist, his art
and this book.*

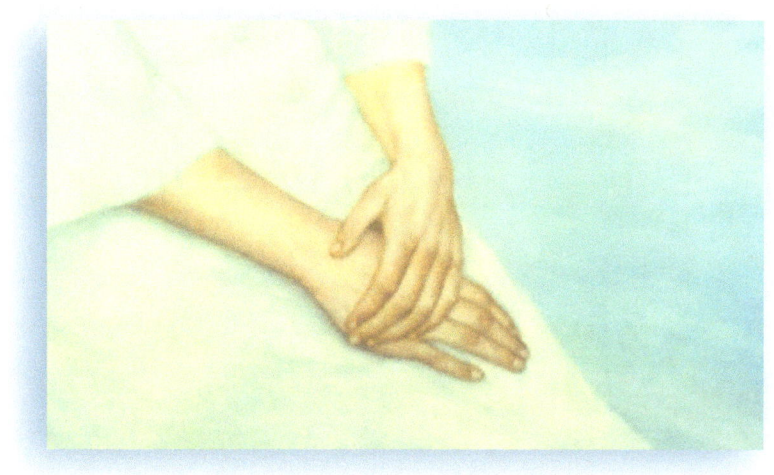

Jesus' Hands

About the Artist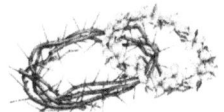

Christian artist, J.L. (Jack) Shively, was born in Wichita, Kansas in 1949. He began his art career at the age of fourteen, copying old master paintings with astonishing precision.

His art became a refuge for him to help escape from a troubled home life. As a result of the turmoil in his home, he began experiencing depression, and at one point he became suicidal. It was at that time a Christian at his school noticed his misery and contributed to his acceptance of Jesus as his Lord and Savior.

The artist received several scholarships. One was from the Art Students League in New York City, which he accepted, glad to have the opportunity to distance himself from the problems in his family.

It was at the Art Students League that he met his future wife, Hannah. Jack led Hannah to the Lord and the couple were married in 1968.

In New York, Jack began making his living as a portrait artist, working in pastels. He later moved with his wife to Long Island where the couple operated their own business, a combination art gallery and gift shop

The artist discovered that he had a unique ability to capture the ocean on canvas, and set about to become the world's greatest seascape painter; but God had other plans for this gifted young artist.

After nine years, the business was sold and the artist and his wife moved to New England. It was there in the quiet solitude of a woodland cabin that the artist turned his work over to the Lord and he began painting portraits of Jesus.

During this time the couple had befriended another couple and went into business with them. However, that business failed and as a result, the Shivelys lost their cherished woodland home. But this apparent disaster was the vehicle the Lord used to launch the couple into ministry.

They returned to Wichita and purchased their first travel trailer and began doing secular art shows as a witness for the Lord. They worked their way to California where the weather would enable them to operate year round. Their camper was their only home and they struggled financially; but at the same time they were always provided with what they needed, sometimes miraculously at the last minute. There were several instances when total strangers would come up to them, hand them much needed funds at just the right time, saying, "The Lord told me to give this to you."

The Shivelys also experienced God's supernatural protection. One time they were prevented from taking a hazardous mountain short cut, when the lights on their truck and trailer suddenly malfunctioned in a way that was technically impossible. This prevented them from making the trip.

It was later discovered that there was nothing wrong with the lights, but their trailer brakes were not working and it would have been impossible to brake their old, heavy trailer on those steep mountain descents.

The couple eventually came to realize that everything that the Lord was allowing them to experience was to build their faith and trust in Him. They believe that this spiritual growth would not have developed if they had remained in their previous "Comfort Zone," before the loss of their house. They truly learned the truth of the scripture that promises "All things work together for good to them that love God, to them who are the called according to His purpose," Romans 8:28.

The Shivelys were now among California's homeless population, along with so many others like them who were living in tents and their cars in state parks where the rent was all they could afford. The result of the Shively's experiences had a profound impact on the artist and he began illustrating the needs he saw around him, expressing the Lord's care for His "Least of These" in dramatic charcoal and pencil illustrations. One of those drawings was utilized on the cover of the LA Mission, "Transformer" publication in 1988.

The artist's sensitive drawings of the poor, prompted one pastor to introduce Jack as, "Mr. Conviction."

The artist began sharing his testimony with his art in 1991, and the couple began ministering in churches. This ministry became fulltime and after nine years in California, the Shivelys traveled back across the country to minister primarily in churches and events on the east coast. This ministry continued for twenty-six years. The Shivelys exhausted a total of five travel trailers over a total of thirty-five years ministering on the road. One of those campers was only a mere seventeen feet, in which the couple lived for seven years.

The culmination of most of the art that was produced over the years in those campers, is now being made available in this book. The artist sees his work as merely vehicles to share God's word and the life giving gospel of the Messiah Jesus.

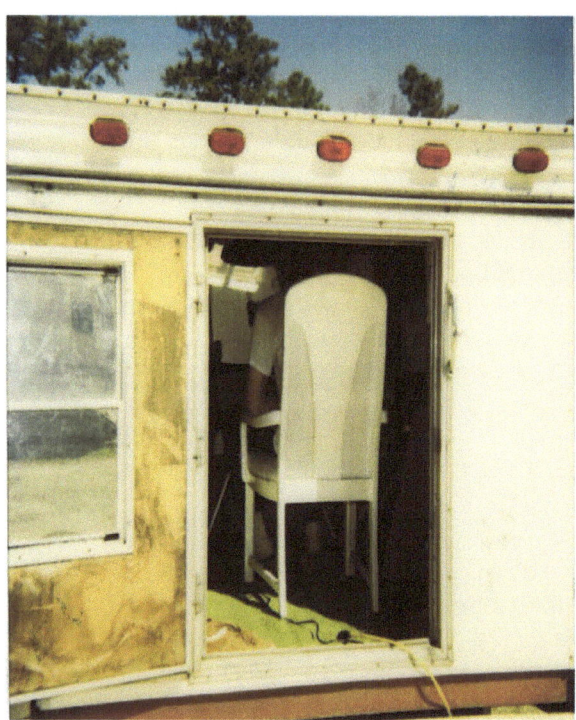

The artist at work in his "Studio;" The shell on the back of his truck.

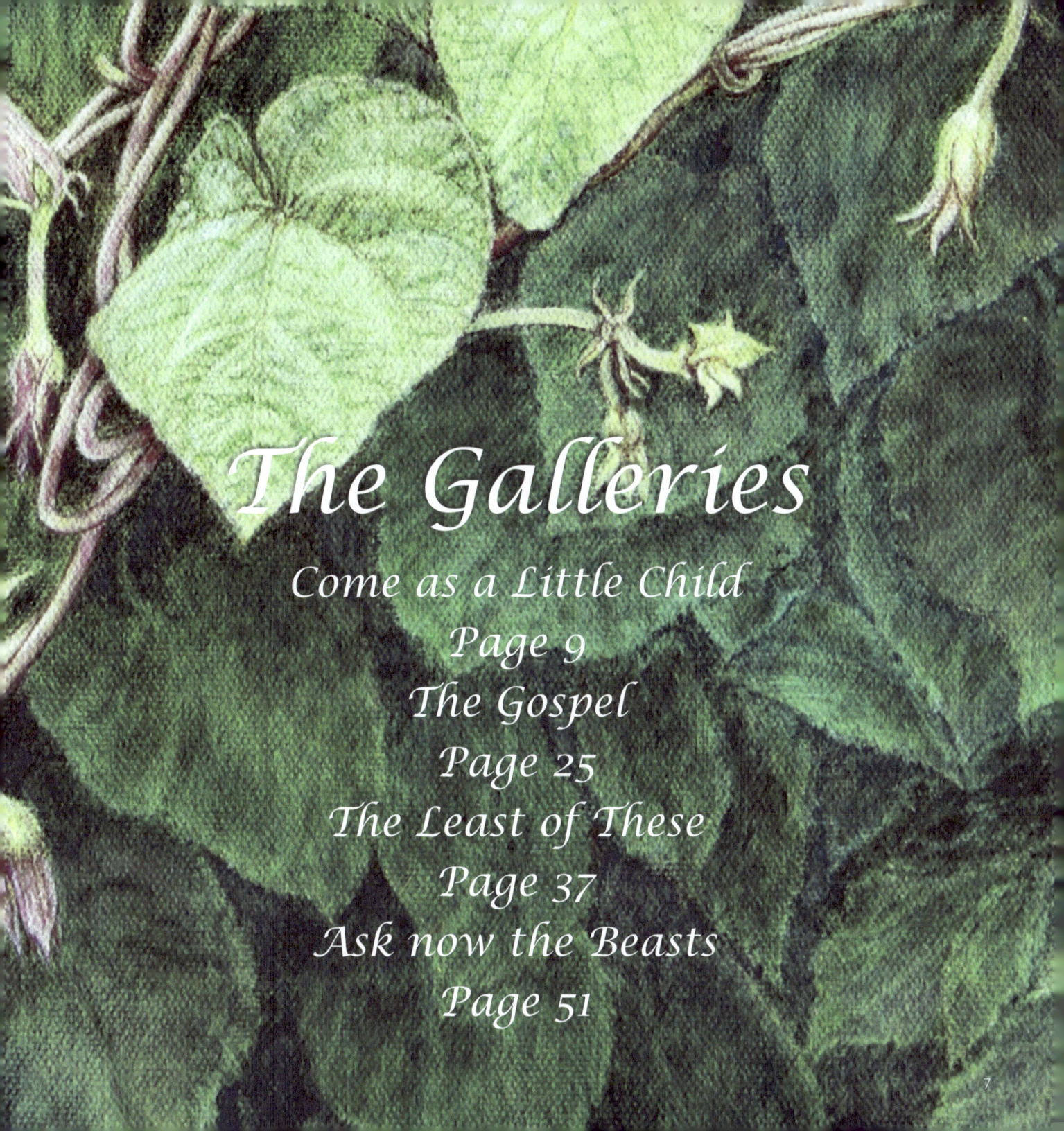

The Galleries

Come as a Little Child
Page 9
The Gospel
Page 25
The Least of These
Page 37
Ask now the Beasts
Page 51

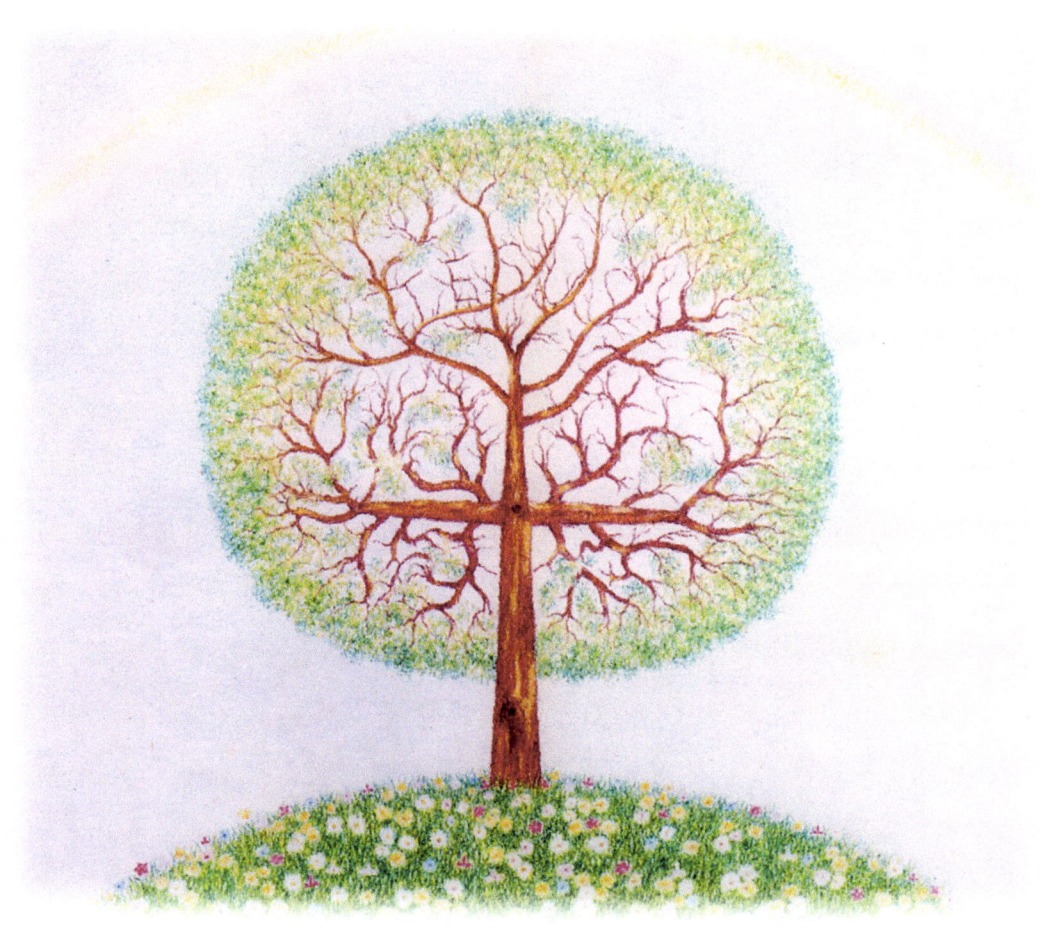

The Jesus Tree

Come as a Little Child

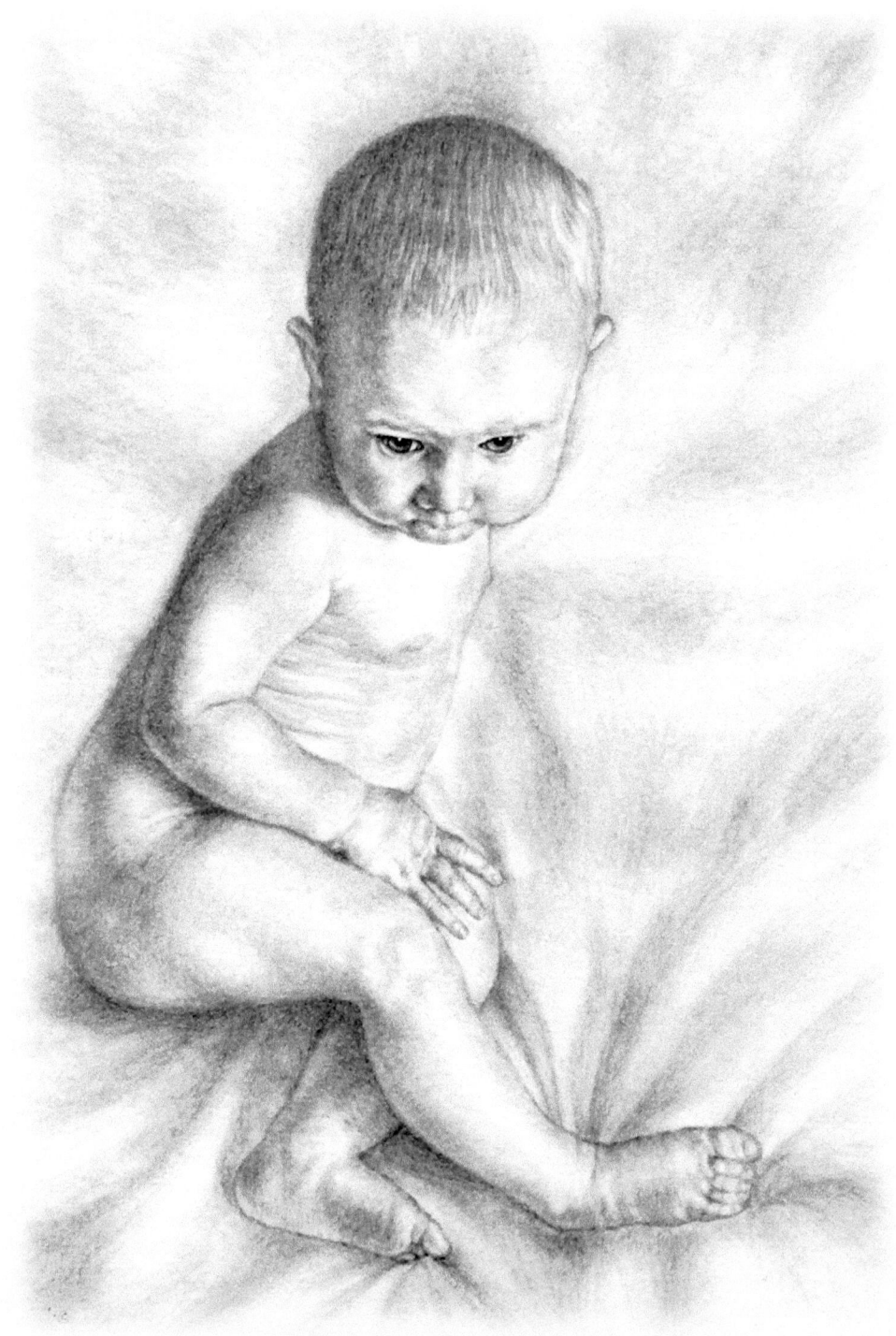

*Therefore
if anyone is in Christ,
he is a new creature:
old things are passed away;
behold, all things are
become new.
II Corinthians 5:17*

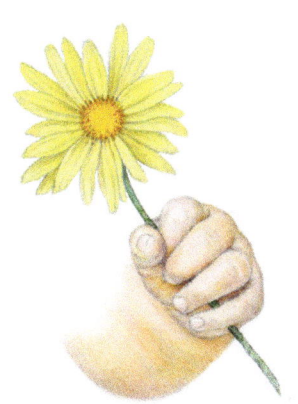

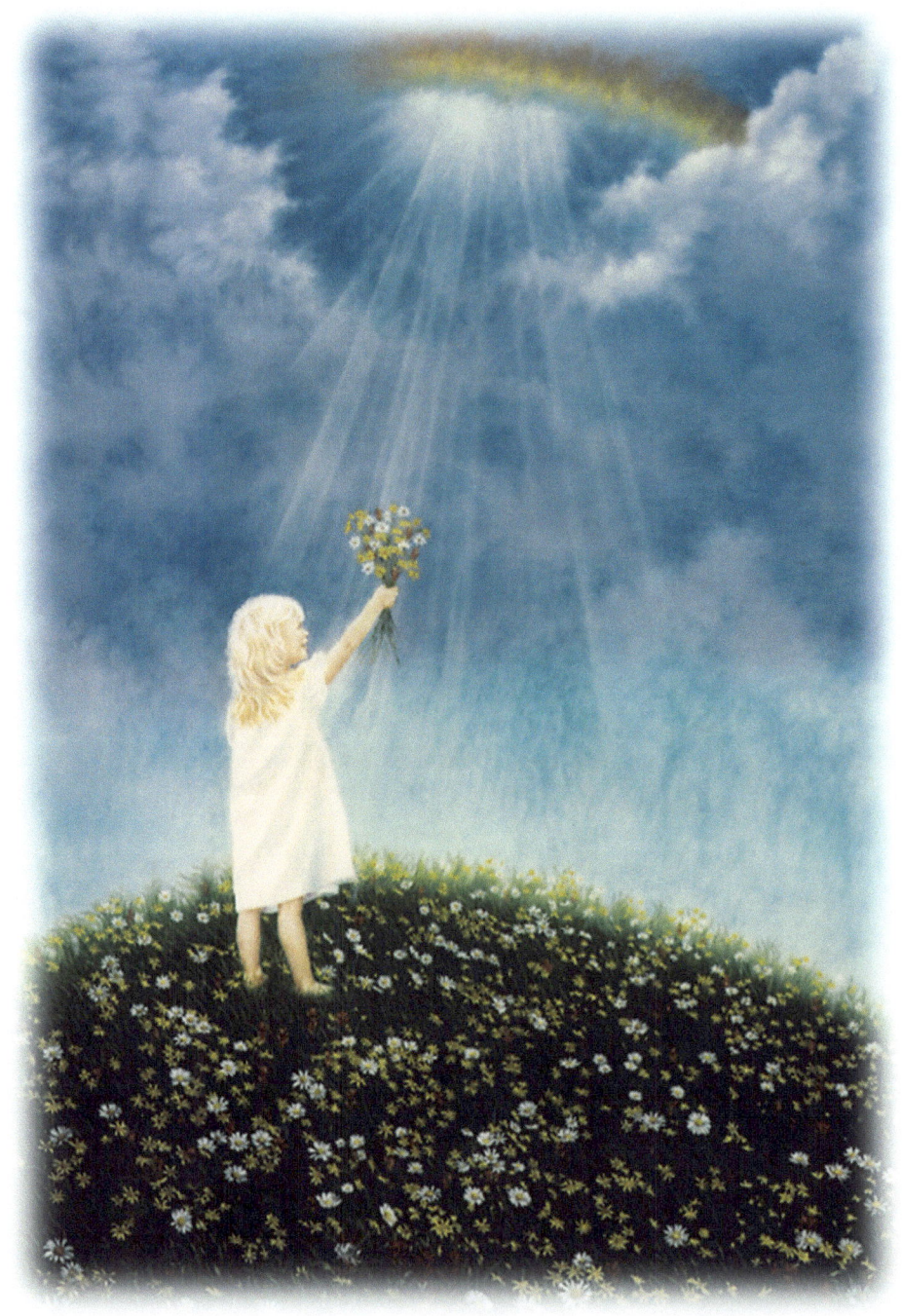

And Jesus said to them, Yes; have you never read, out of the mouth of babes and infants You have perfected praise?
Matthew 21:16

And whoever shall receive one such little child in My name receives Me.
Matthew 18:5

*Truly
I say to you,
whoever shall
not receive the
kingdom of God
as a little child
shall in no way
enter into it.
Luke 18:17*

*Whoever
therefore shall
humble himself as
this little child,
the same is
greatest in the
kingdom of heaven.
Matthew 18:4*

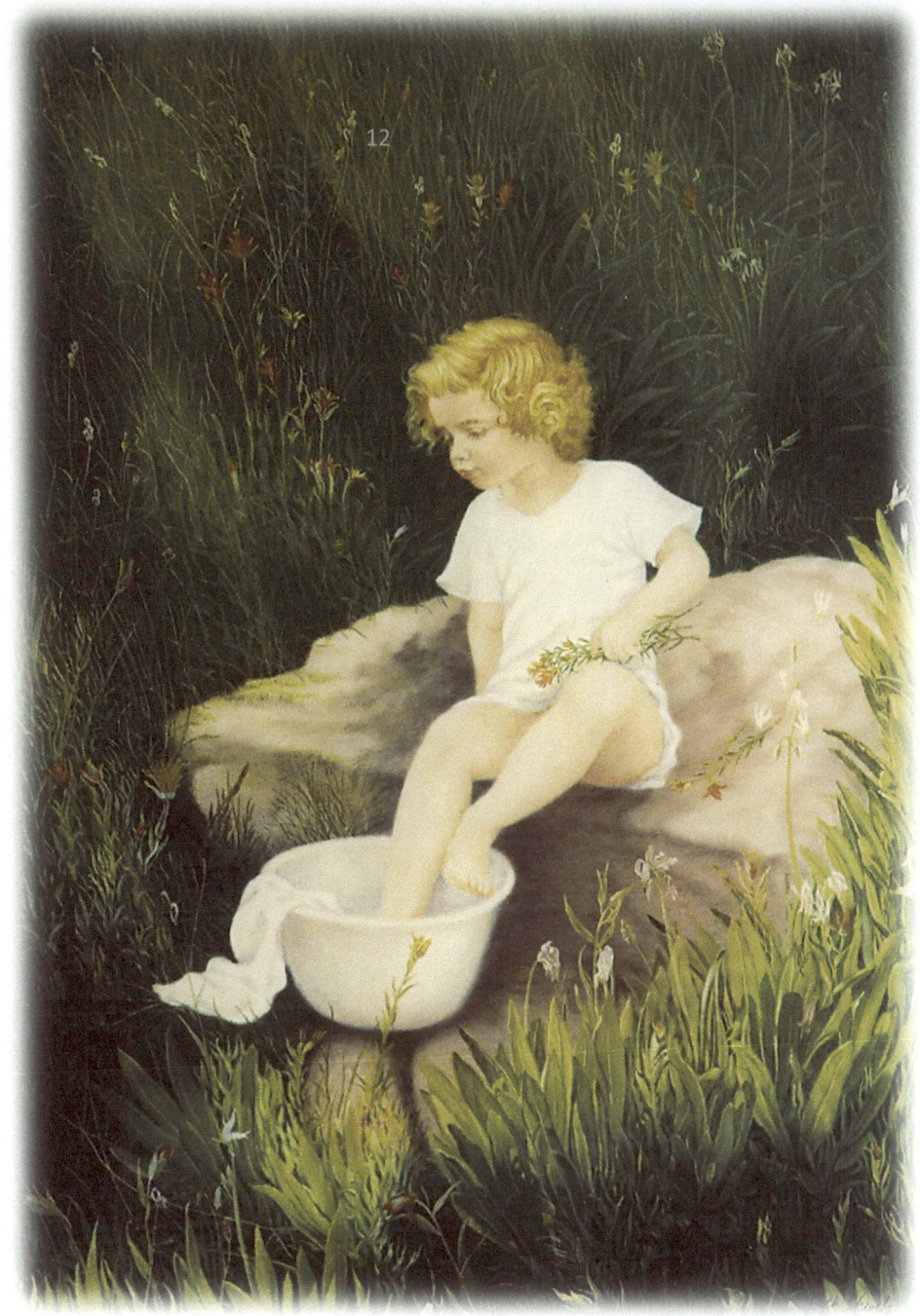

Who shall separate us from the Love of Christ?

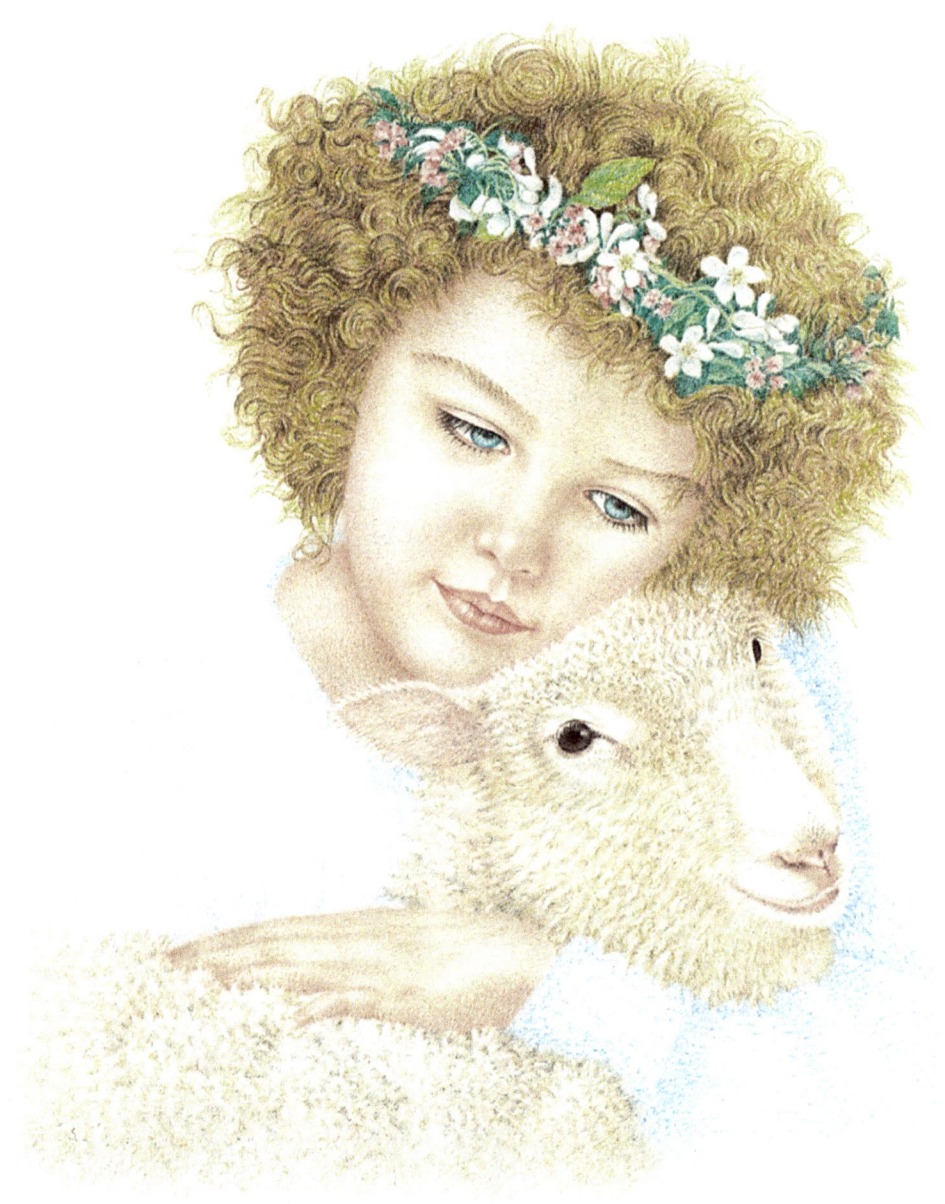

*Shall tribulation,
or distress, or persecution,
or famine,
or nakedness, or peril,
or sword?
As it is written,
for Your sake we are
killed all the day long;
we are accounted as
sheep for the slaughter.
Yet, in all these things we are
more than conquerors
through Him that loved us.
For I am persuaded, that neither death,
nor life, nor angels,
nor principalities, nor powers,
nor things present, nor things to come,
nor height, nor depth, nor any other creature,
shall be able to separate us from the love of God,
which is in Christ Jesus our Lord.
Romans 8:35-39*

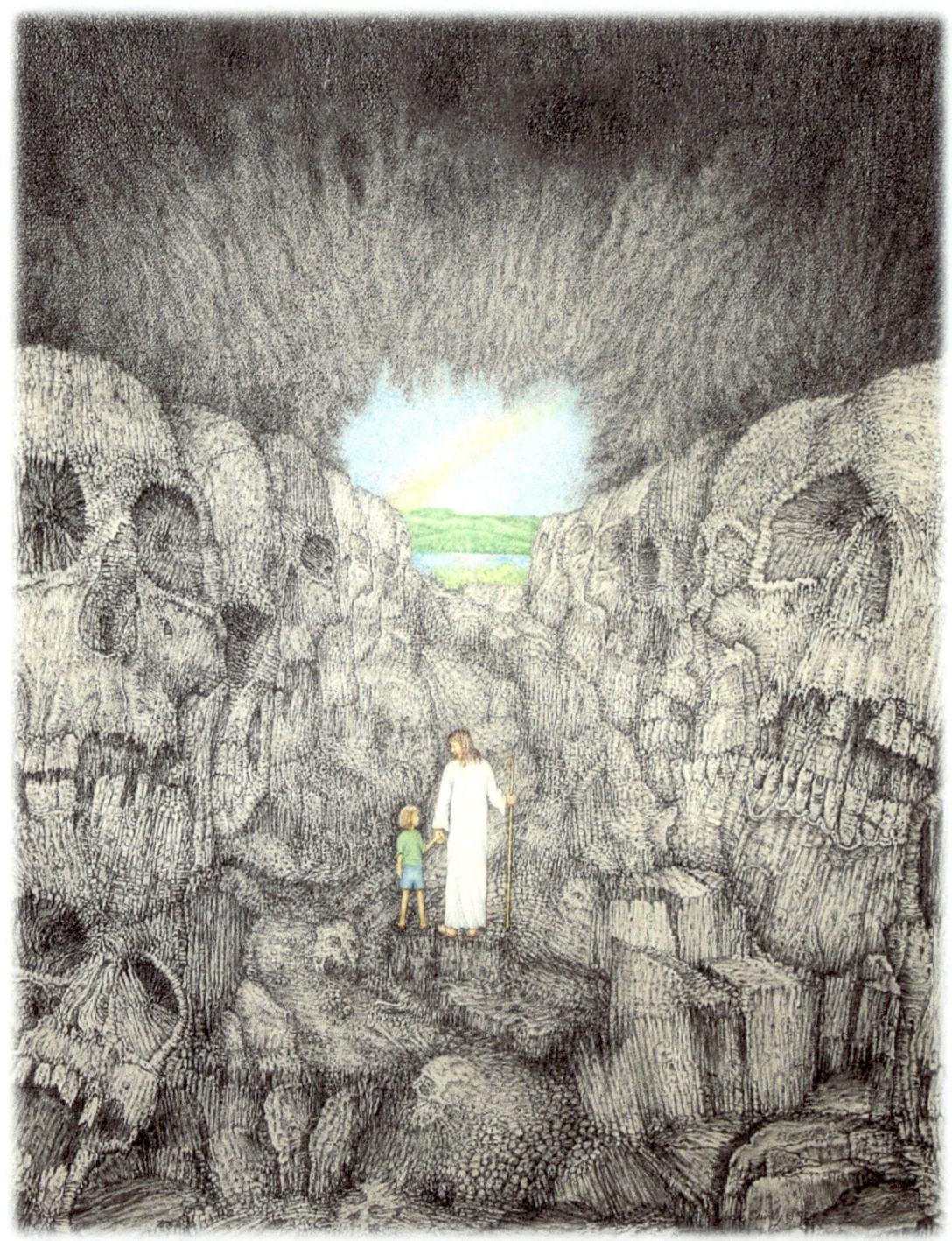

Psalm 23

The LORD is my shepherd; I shall not want.
He makes me to lie down in green pastures:
He leads me beside the still waters.
He restores my soul:
He leads me in the paths of righteousness
for His name's sake.
Yes, though I walk through
the valley of the shadow of death,
I will fear no evil: for You are with me;
Your rod and Your staff they comfort me.
You prepare a table before me
in the presence of my enemies:
You anoint my head with oil; my cup runs over.
Surely goodness and mercy shall follow me
all the days of my life:
and I will dwell in the house of
the LORD forever.

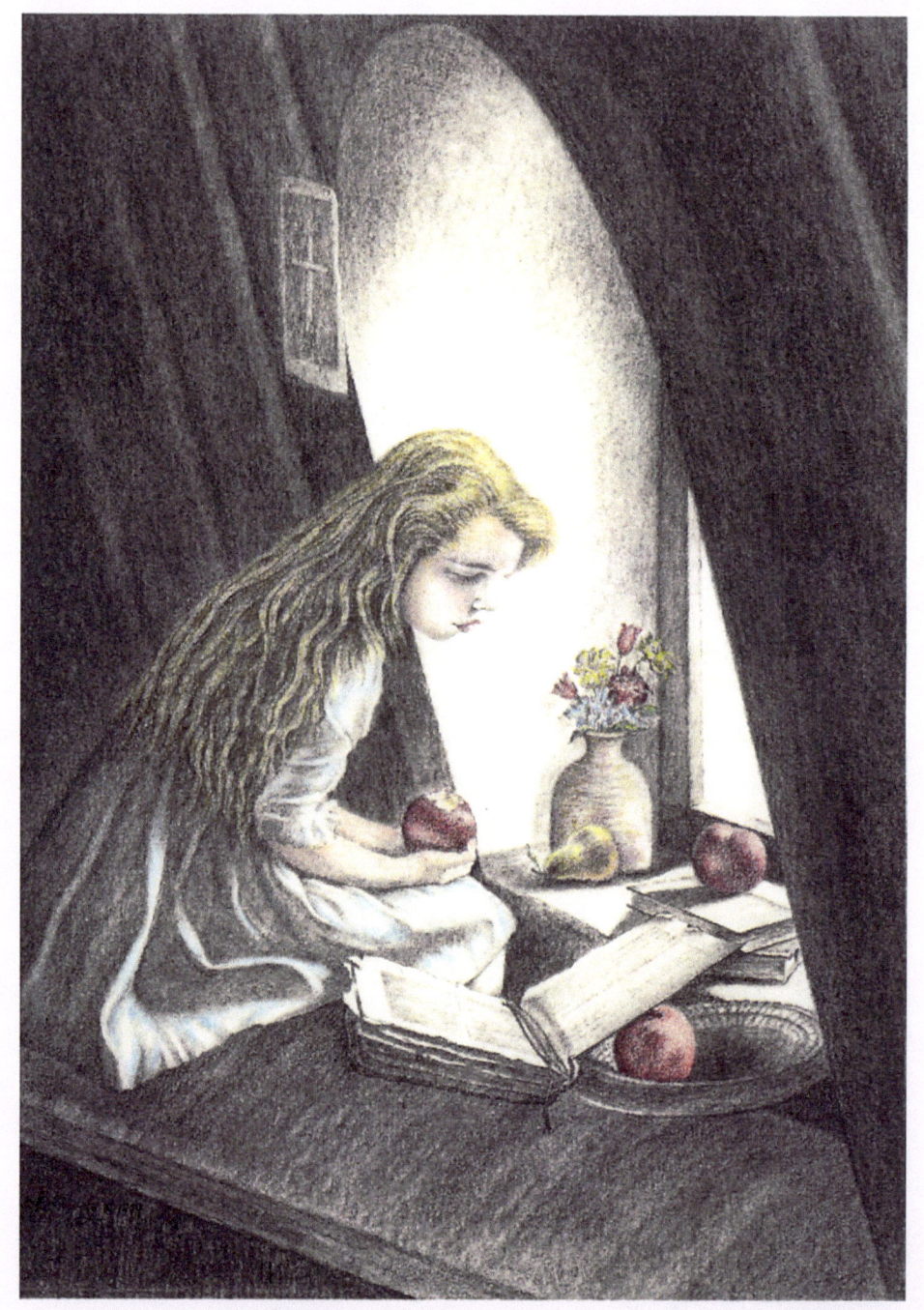

*You seek out of the book of the Lord and read,
no one of these shall fail...Isaiah 34:16*

*Knowing this first,
that no prophecy of the Scripture is of any private interpretation. For the prophecy came not in old time by the will of man: but the holy men of God spoke as they were moved by the Holy Spirit.
II Peter 1:20, 21
All Scripture is given by inspiration of God, and is profitable for doctrine, for reproof, for correction, for instruction in righteousness: that the man of God may be perfect, thoroughly furnished to all good works.
II Timothy 3:16, 17
Study to show yourself approved to God,
a workman that needs not to be ashamed,
rightly dividing the word of truth.
II Timothy 2:15
If you continue in My word, then you are My disciples indeed.
and you shall know the truth,
and the truth shall make you free.
John 8:31, 32*

Whatever things are True,
Whatever things are Honest,
Whatever things are Just,
Whatever things are Pure,
Whatever things are Lovely,
Whatever things are of Good report;
If there be any Virtue,
And of there be any Praise ...

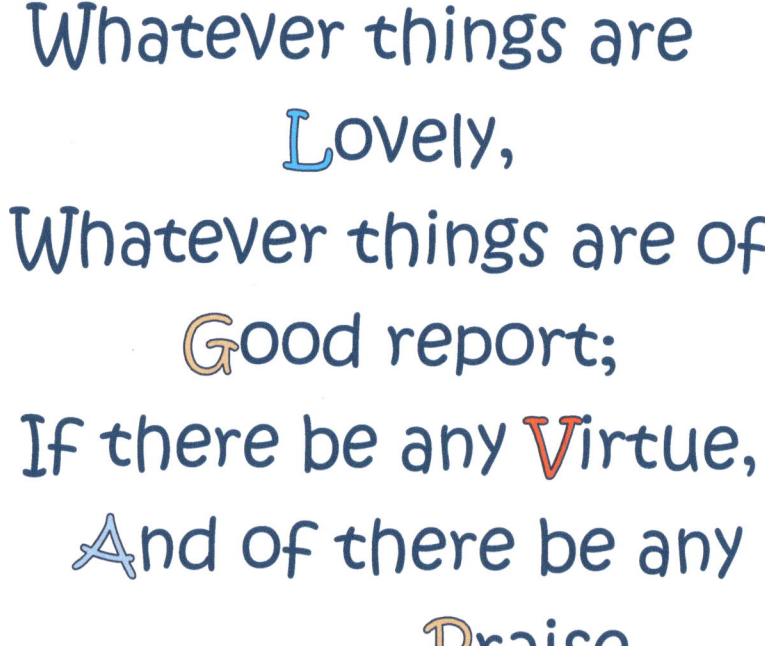

Think on these things...
Philippians 4:8

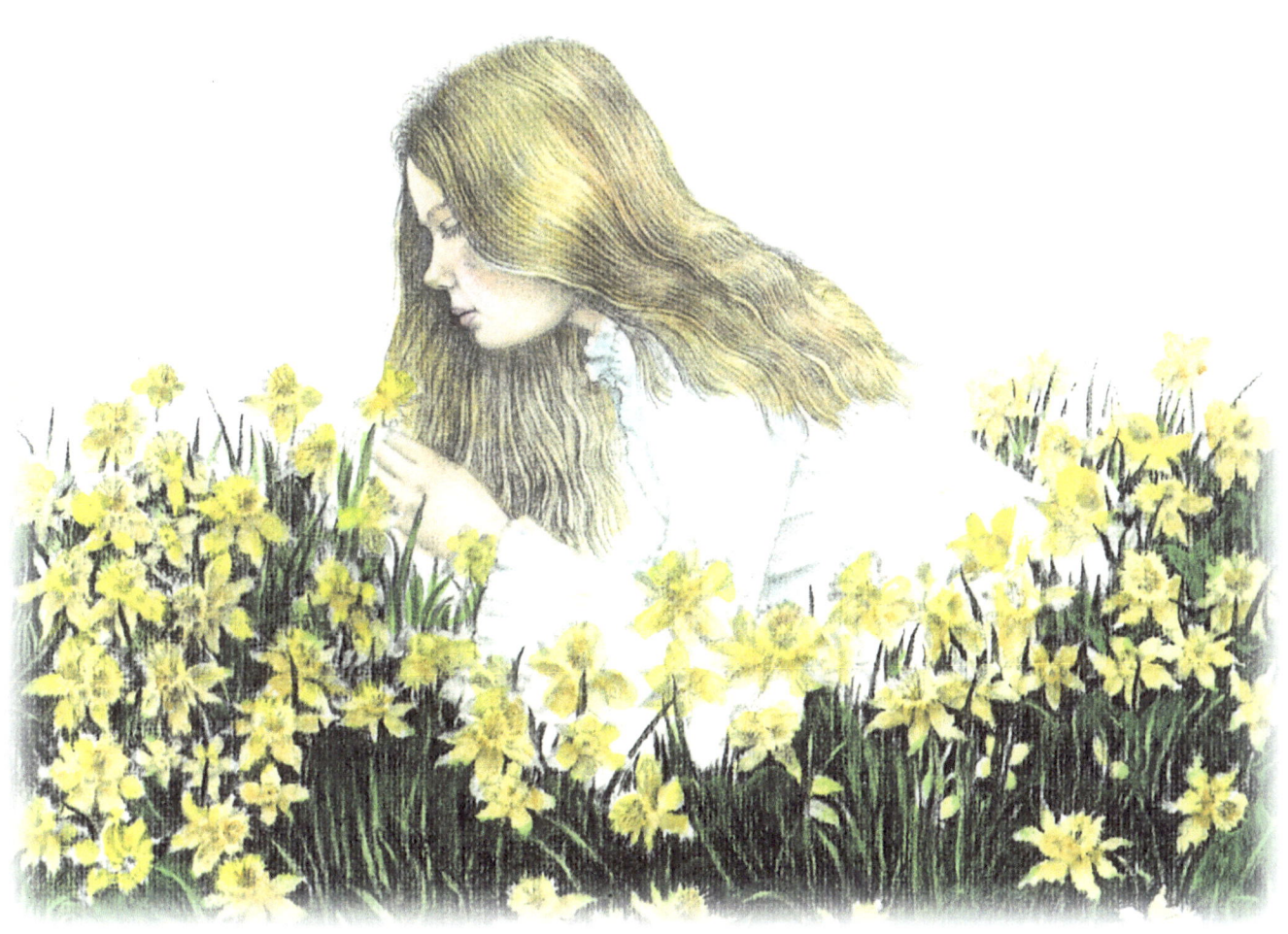

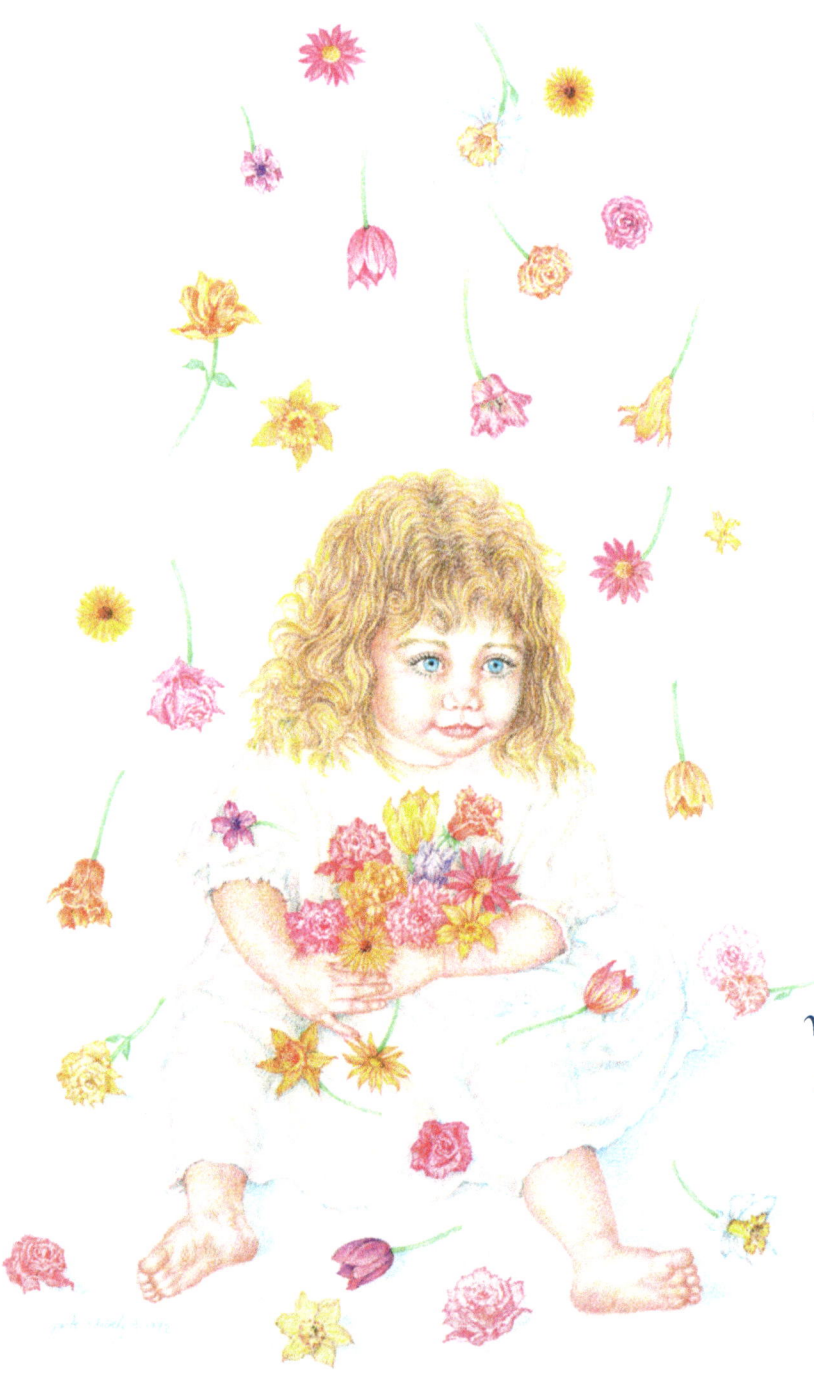

*You are
blessed
of the LORD
which made heaven
and earth.
Psalm 115:15
Every
good gift
and every perfect
gift is from above,
and comes down
from the
Father of lights,
with whom is no
variableness, neither
shadow of turning.
James 1:17*

The LORD
shall fight for you,
and you shall hold
your peace.
Exodus 14:14

Peace
I leave with you,
My peace I give to
you: not as the
world gives,
give I to you.
Let not
your heart be
troubled, neither
let it be afraid.
John 14:27

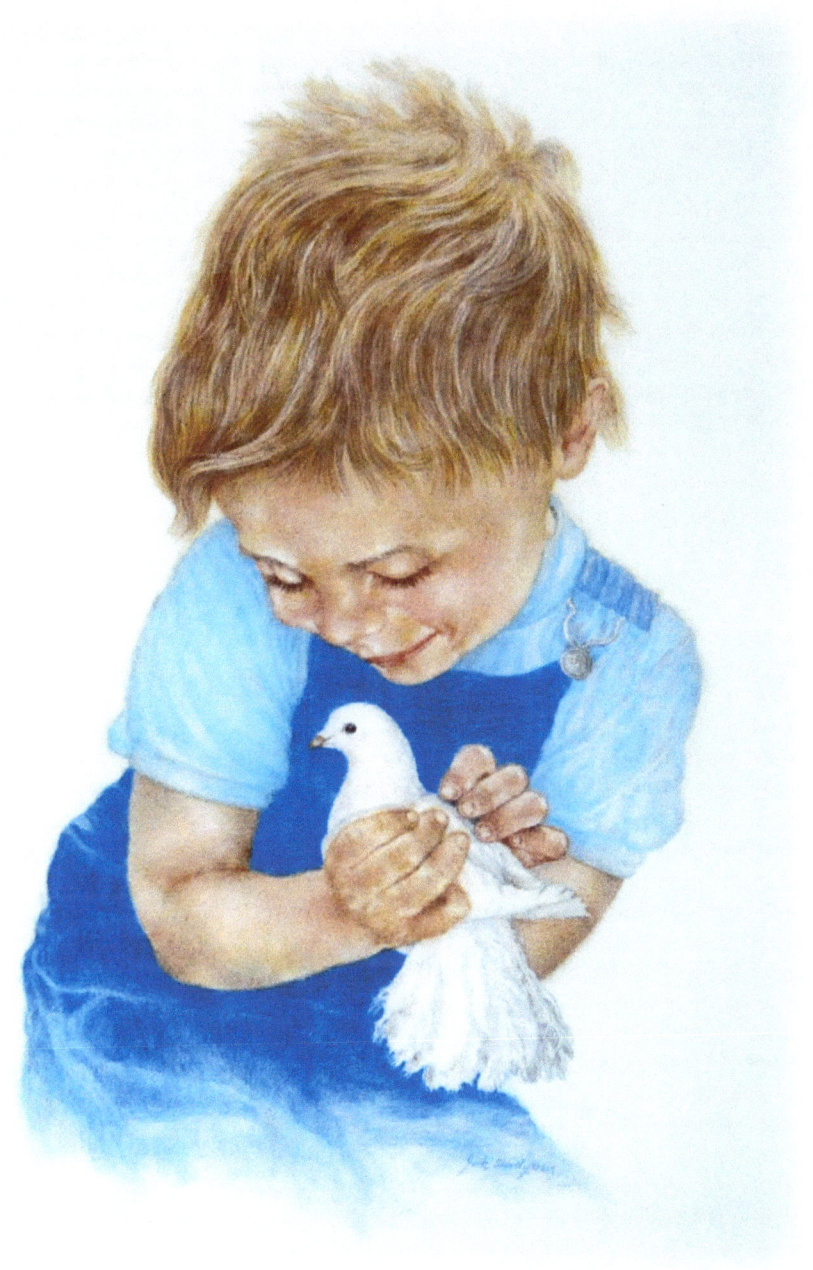

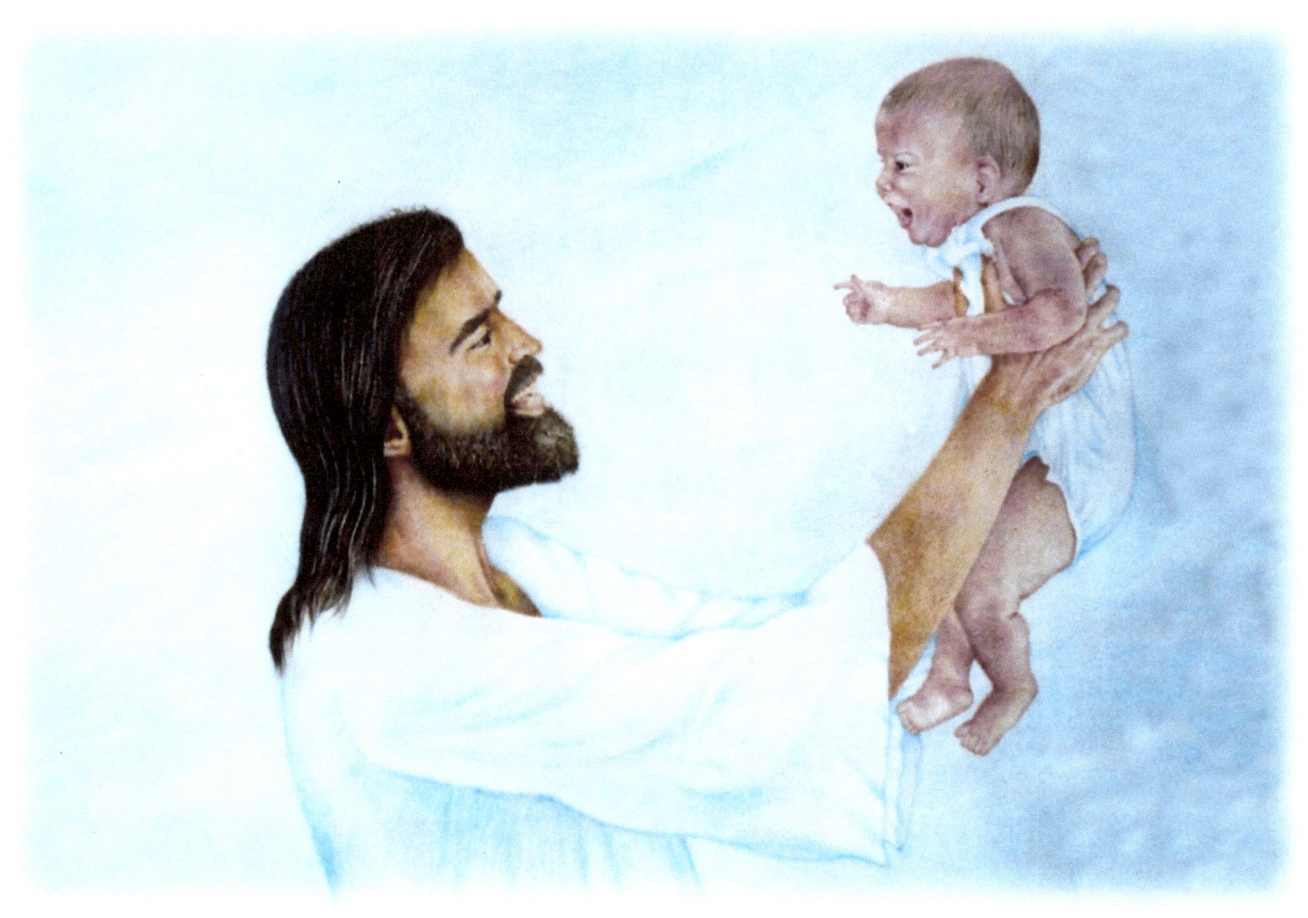

The eternal God is your refuge, and underneath are the everlasting arms...
Deuteronomy 33:27

The Gospel

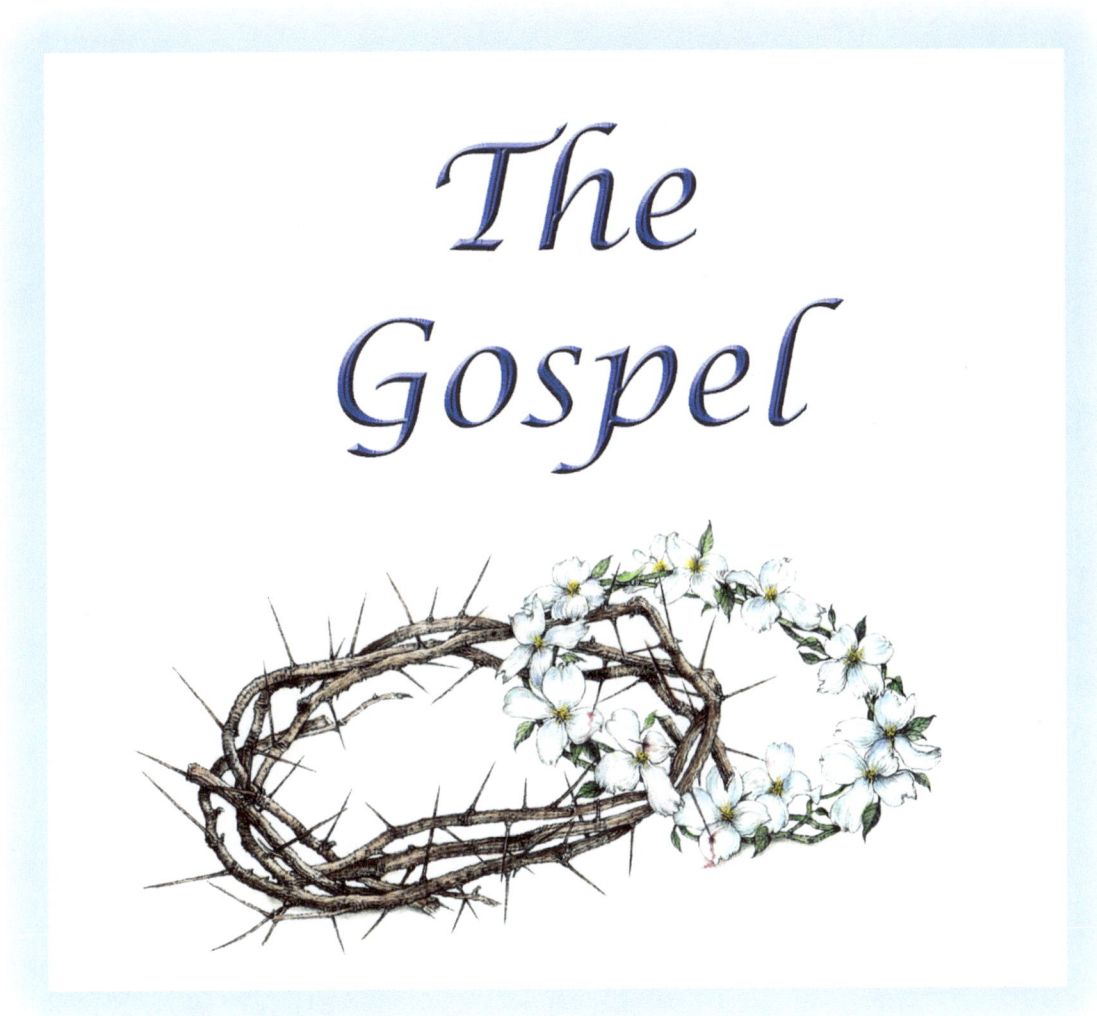

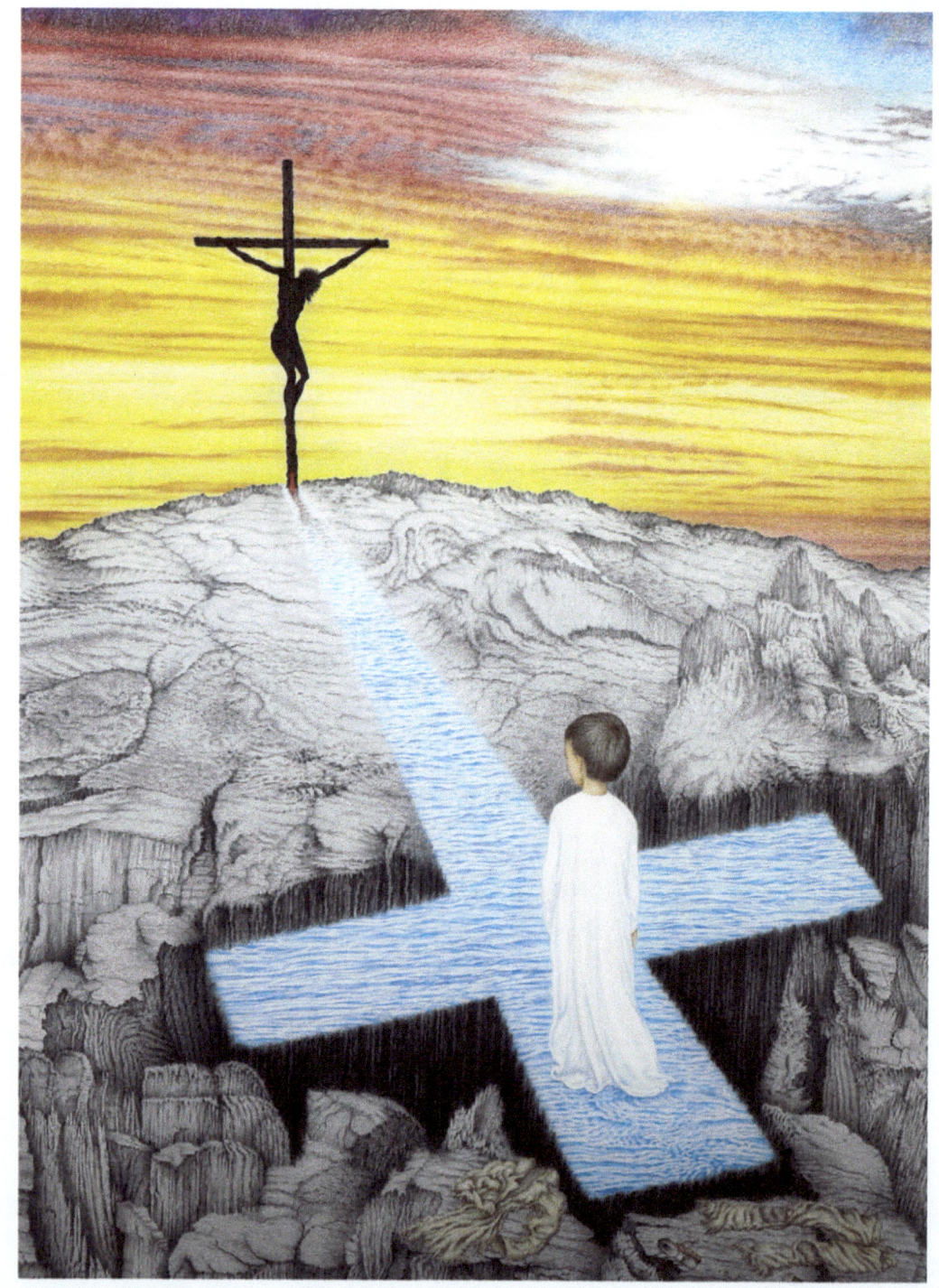

*The word
is near you, even in your mouth,
and in your heart:
that is the word of faith, which we preach;
that if you shall confess with your mouth
the Lord Jesus, and shall believe
in your heart that God has raised Him
from the dead, you shall be saved.
Romans 10:8,9*

*For by grace
you are saved through faith;
and that not of yourselves: it is the gift of God:
not of works, lest any man should boast.
For we are His workmanship, created
in Christ Jesus to good works,
which God has before ordained that
we should walk in them.
Ephesians 2:8-10*

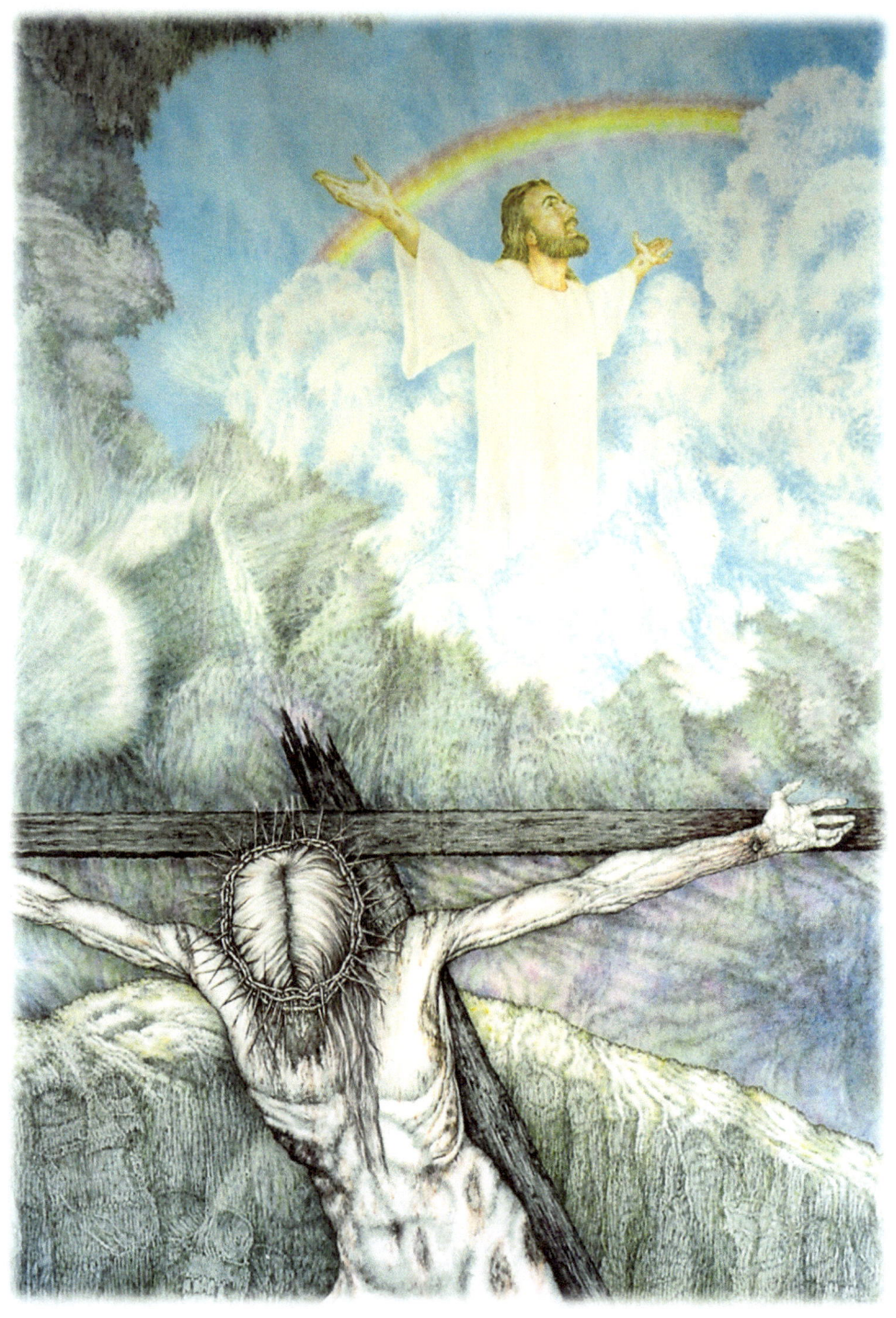

I am the resurrection, and the life: he that believes in Me, though he may die, yet shall he live: and whoever lives and believes in Me shall never die. Do you believe this?

John 11:25,26

I am
the way, the truth,
and the life:
no one comes
to the Father,
but by Me.
John 14:6

Come to Me,
all you that labor
and are heavy laden,
and I will give you
rest.
Take my yok
upon you,
and learn from Me;
for I am meek
and lowly in heart:
and you shall find
rest to your souls.
For My yoke is easy,
and My burden is
light.
Matthew 11:28 - 30

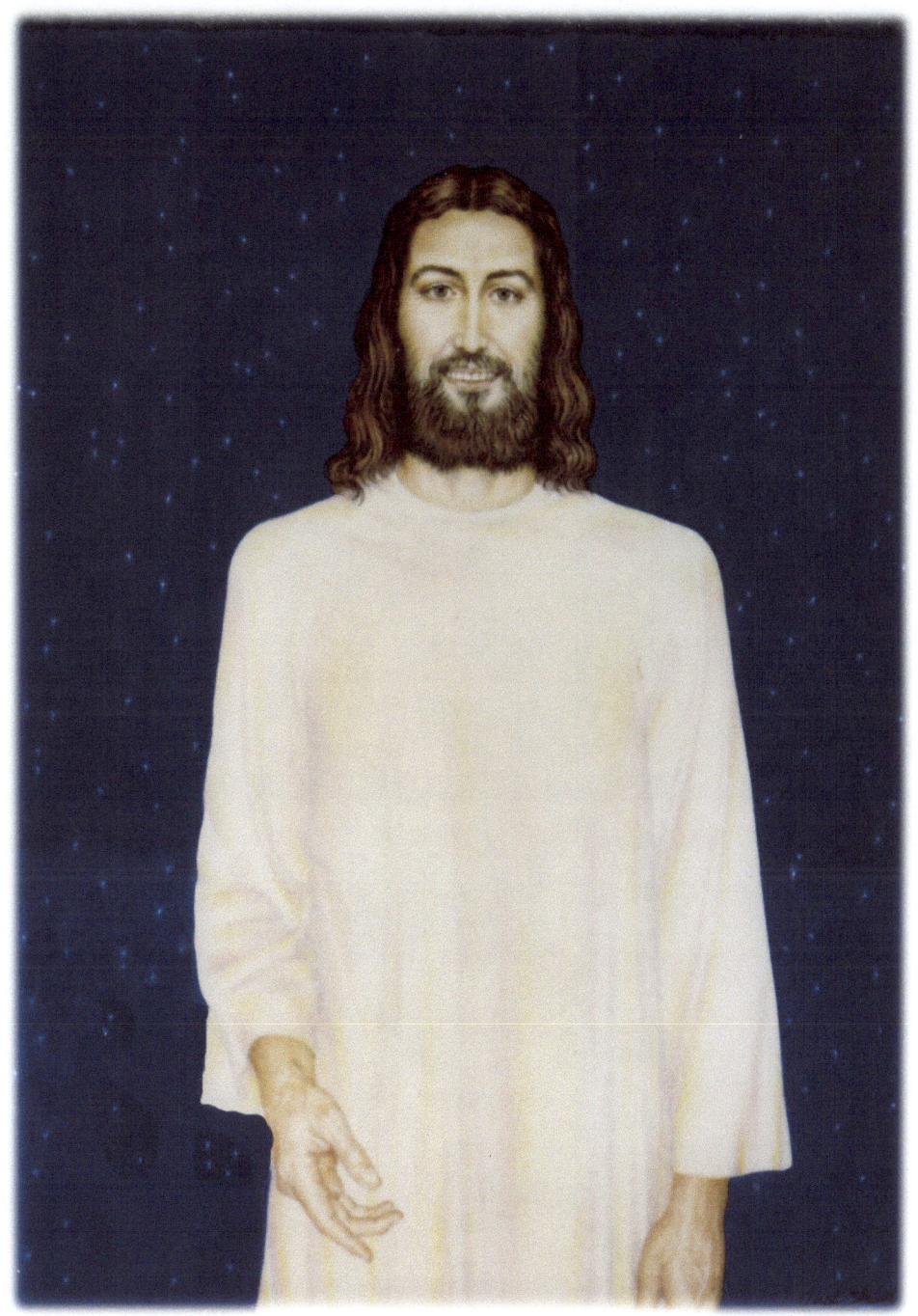

And blessed is he, whoever shall not be offended in Me.
Matthew 11:6

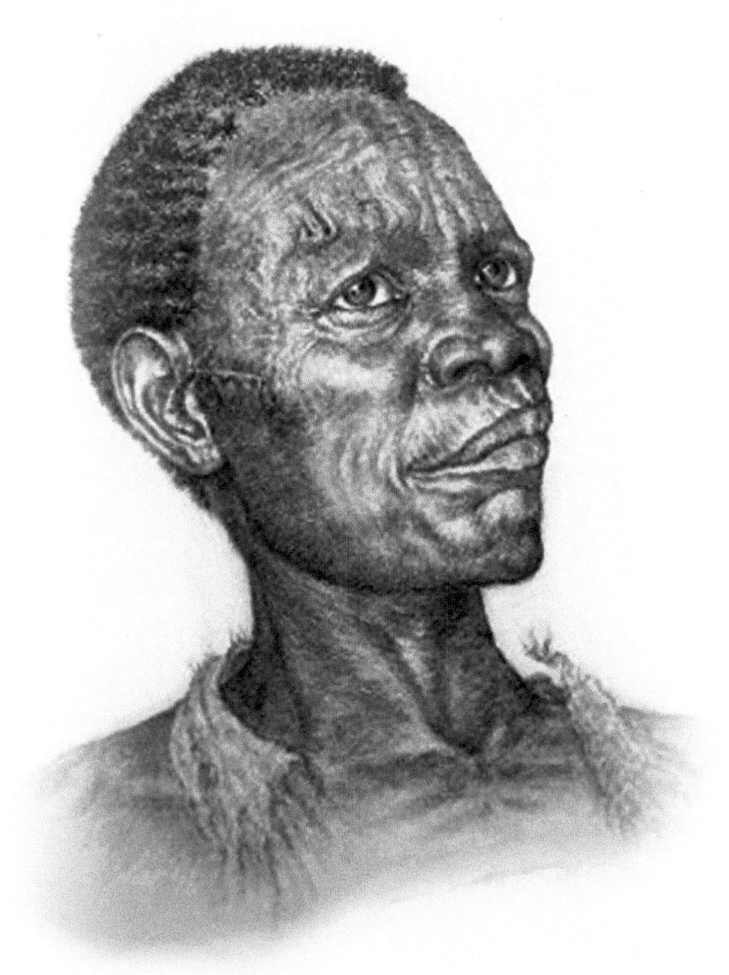

Blessed
are they which are persecuted for righteousness' sake:
for theirs is the kingdom of heaven.
Matthew 5:10

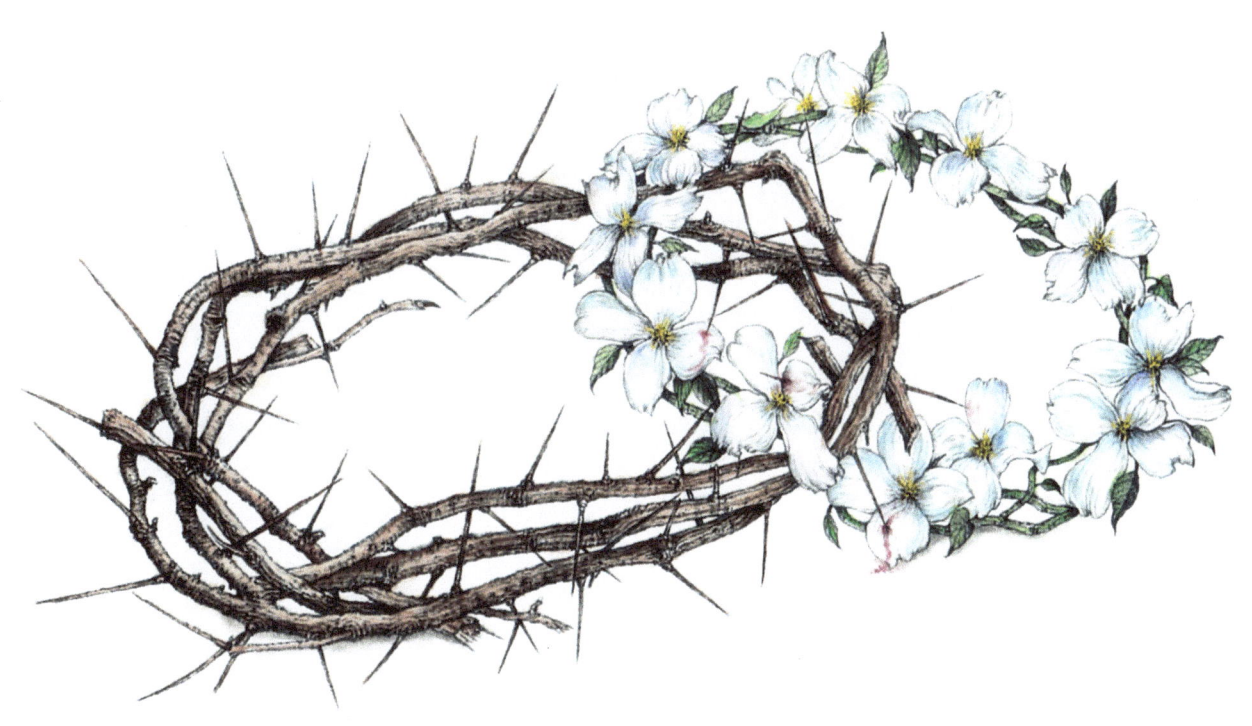

Remember

*Remember them that are in bonds, as bound with them;
and them which suffer adversity,
as being yourselves also in the body.
Hebrews 13:3*

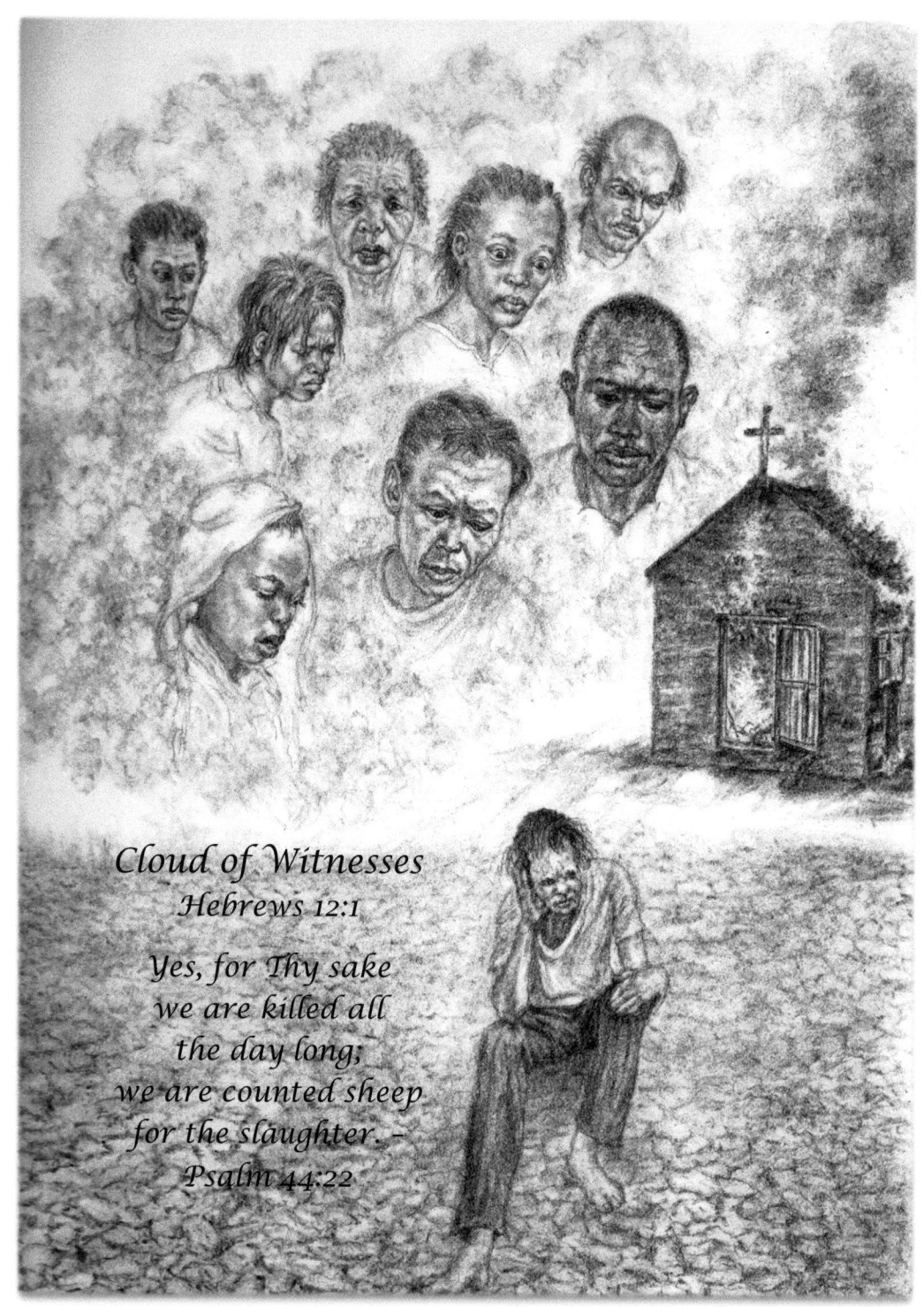

Prayer of the Persecuted

O LORD my God,
In Thee do I put my trust; save me from all them that persecute me and deliver me.

O God, the proud are risen against me, and the assemblies of violent men have sought after my soul; and have not set you before them.

They break in pieces Your people O LORD, and afflict Your heritage.

But the LORD is my defense; and my God is the rock of my refuge.
Deliver me, o my God, out of the hand of the wicked, out of the unrighteous and cruel man.
For You are my hope, o Lord GOD: You are my trust from my youth.

Hear me, o LORD; for Your lovingkindness is good; turn to me according to the multitude of Your tender mercies, and do not hide Your face from Your servant, for I am in trouble: hear me speedily.

Draw near to my soul, and redeem it; deliver my soul because of my enemies.

Blessed be God who has not turned away my prayer, nor His mercy from me.

Psalm 7:1, 86:14, 94:5,22, 71:4,5, 69:16-18, 66:20

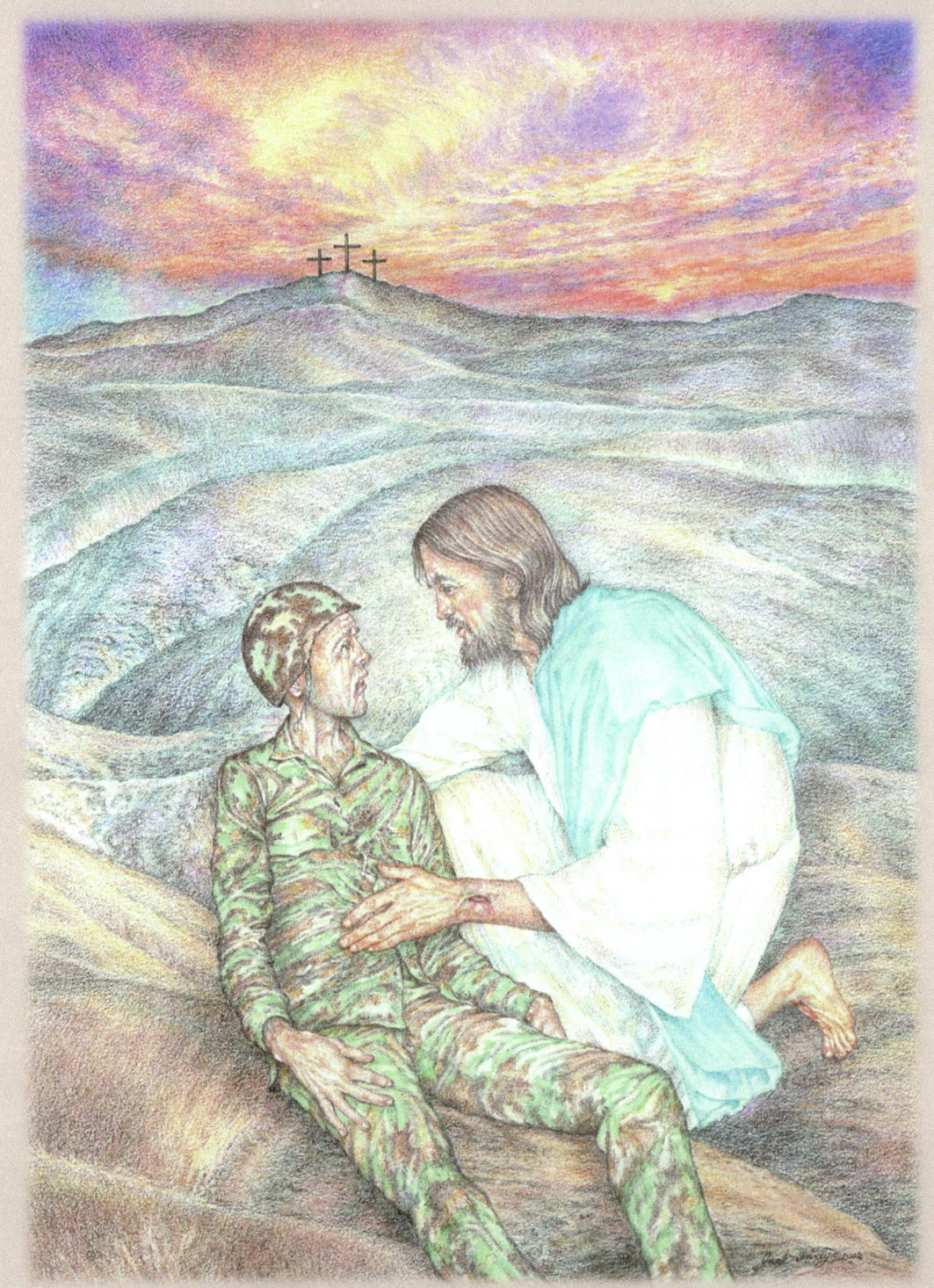

*Blessed are you,
when men shall revile you, and persecute you,
and shall say all manner of evil against you
falsely, for My sake. Rejoice, and be exceedingly
glad: for great is your reward in heaven:
for so they persecuted the prophets
which were before you.
Matthew 5:11,12
These things I have spoken to you, that in Me
you might have peace. In the world you shall
have tribulation: but be of good cheer;
I have overcome the world.
John 16:33
If the world hates you, you know that it
hated Me before it hated you.
John 15:18
Yes, and all that will live godly in Christ Jesus
shall suffer persecution.
II Timothy 3:12
You therefore endure hardness, as a good soldier
of Jesus Christ.
II Timothy 2:3*

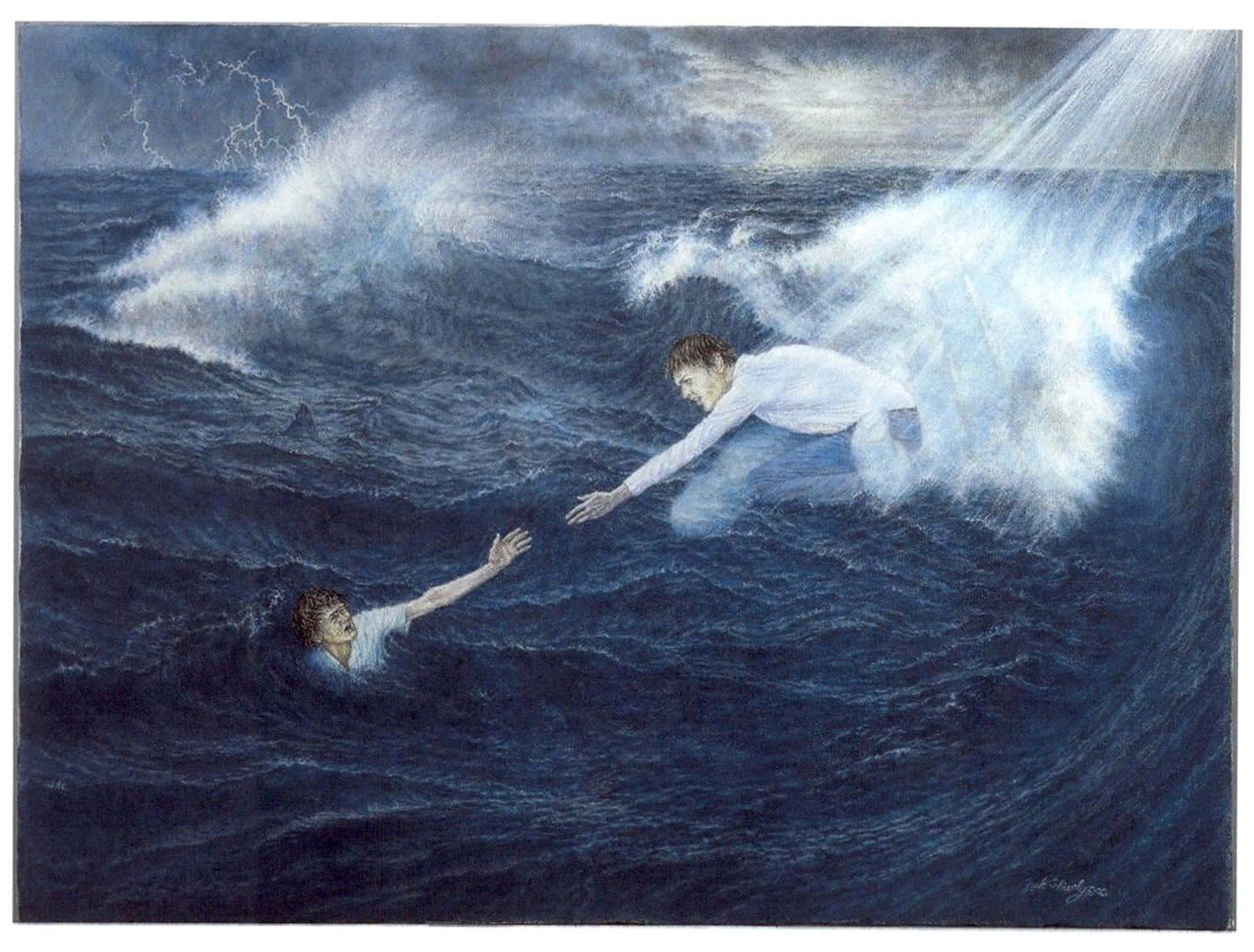

The Evangelist
The time is fulfilled, and the kingdom of God is at hand: you repent, and believe the gospel.
Mark 1:15

The Least of These

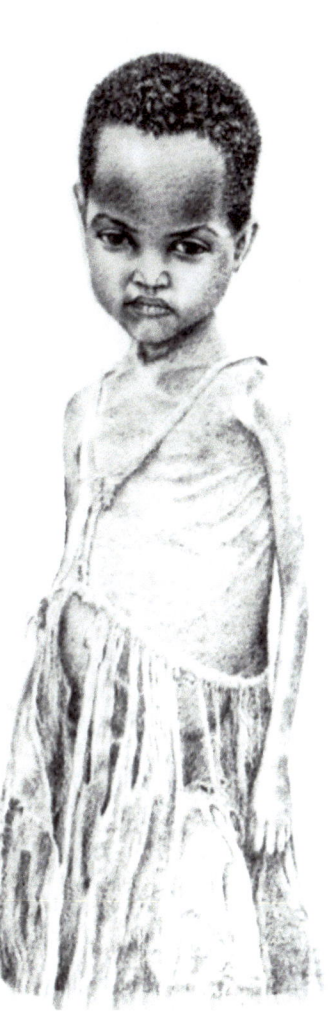

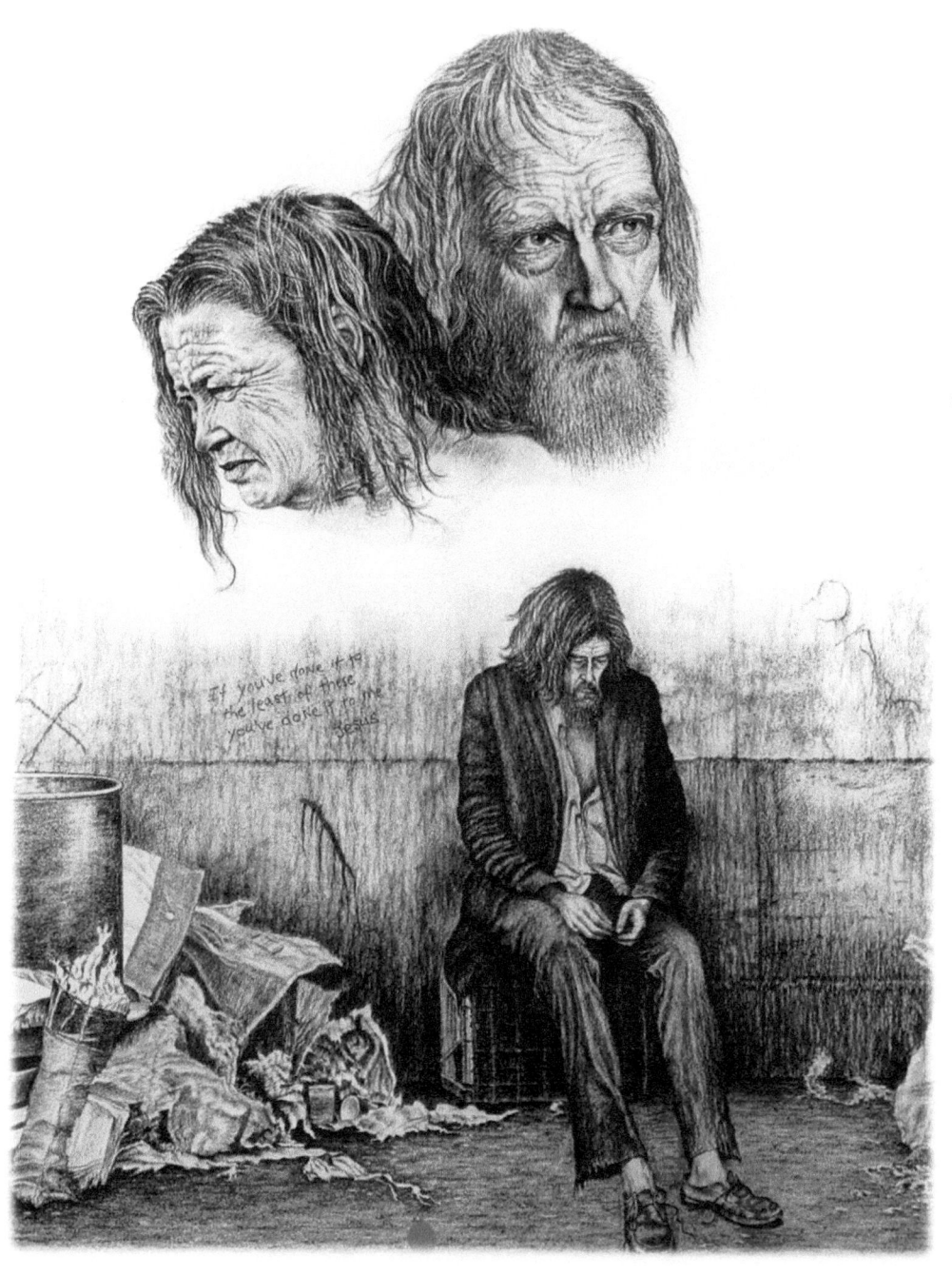

The Spirit of the Lord is upon me, because He has anointed me to preach the gospel to the poor;...

...He has sent me to heal the broken-hearted,...

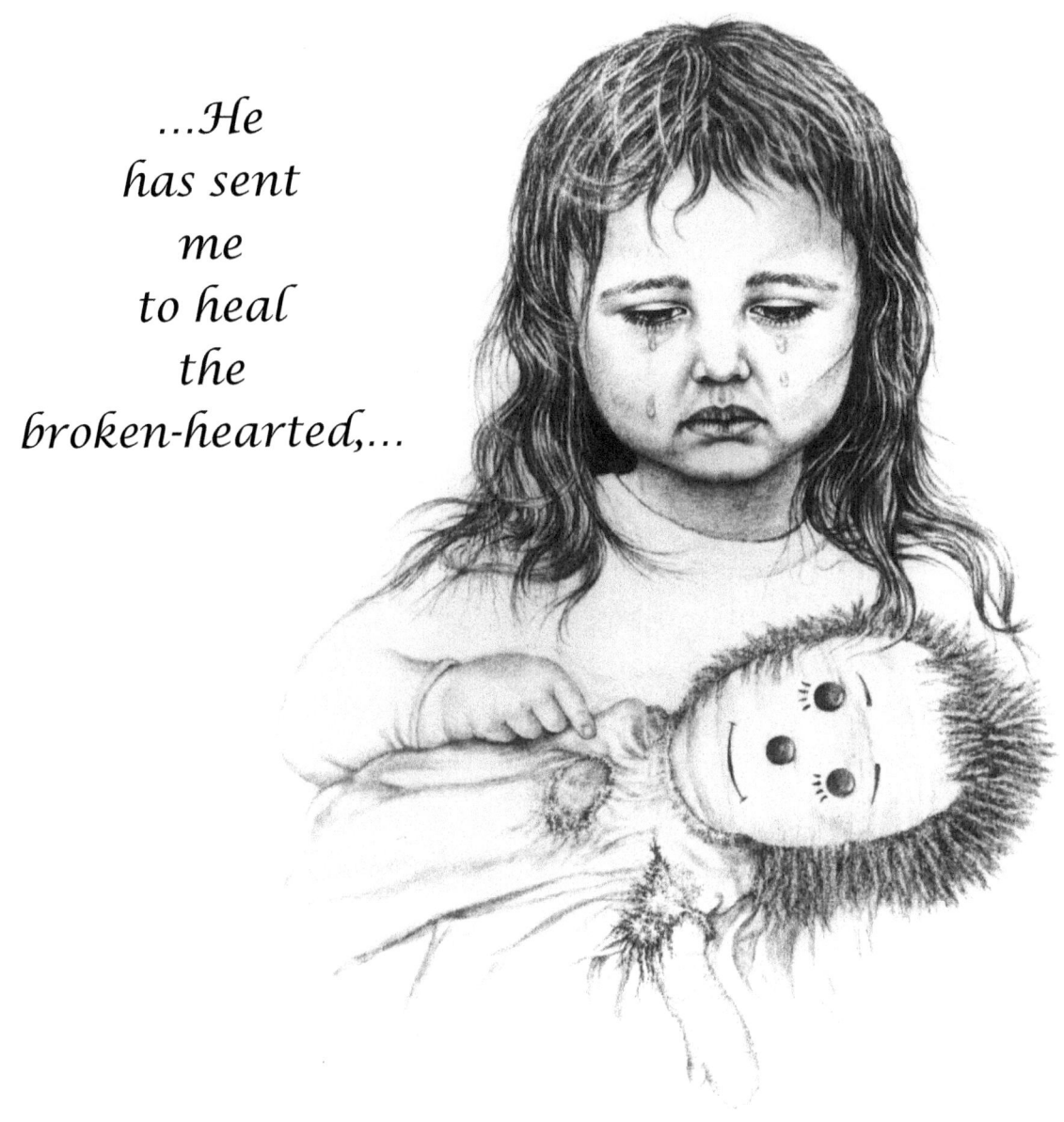

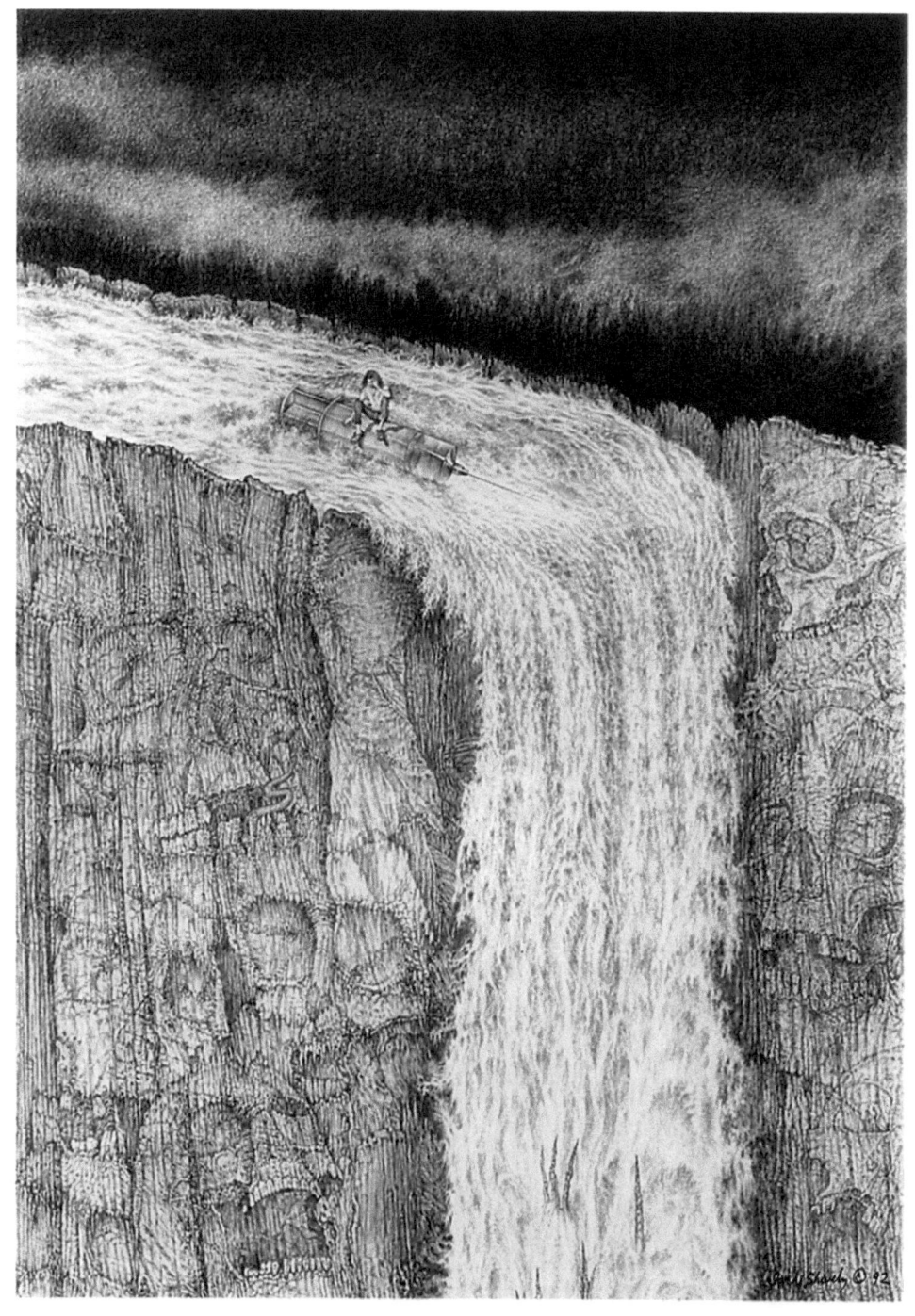

...to preach deliverance to the captives,...

...and recovering of sight to the blind,...

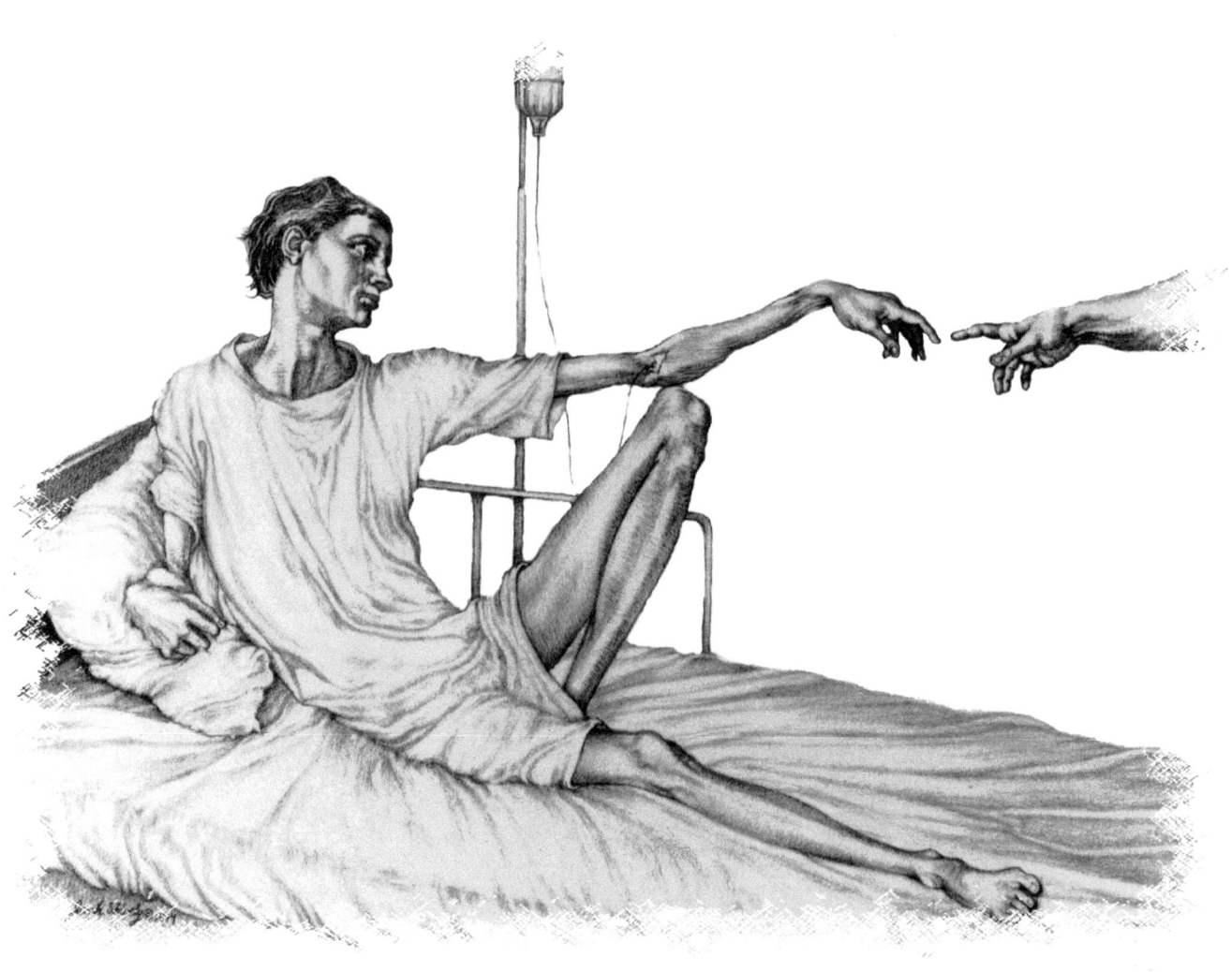

...to set at liberty them that are bruised,...

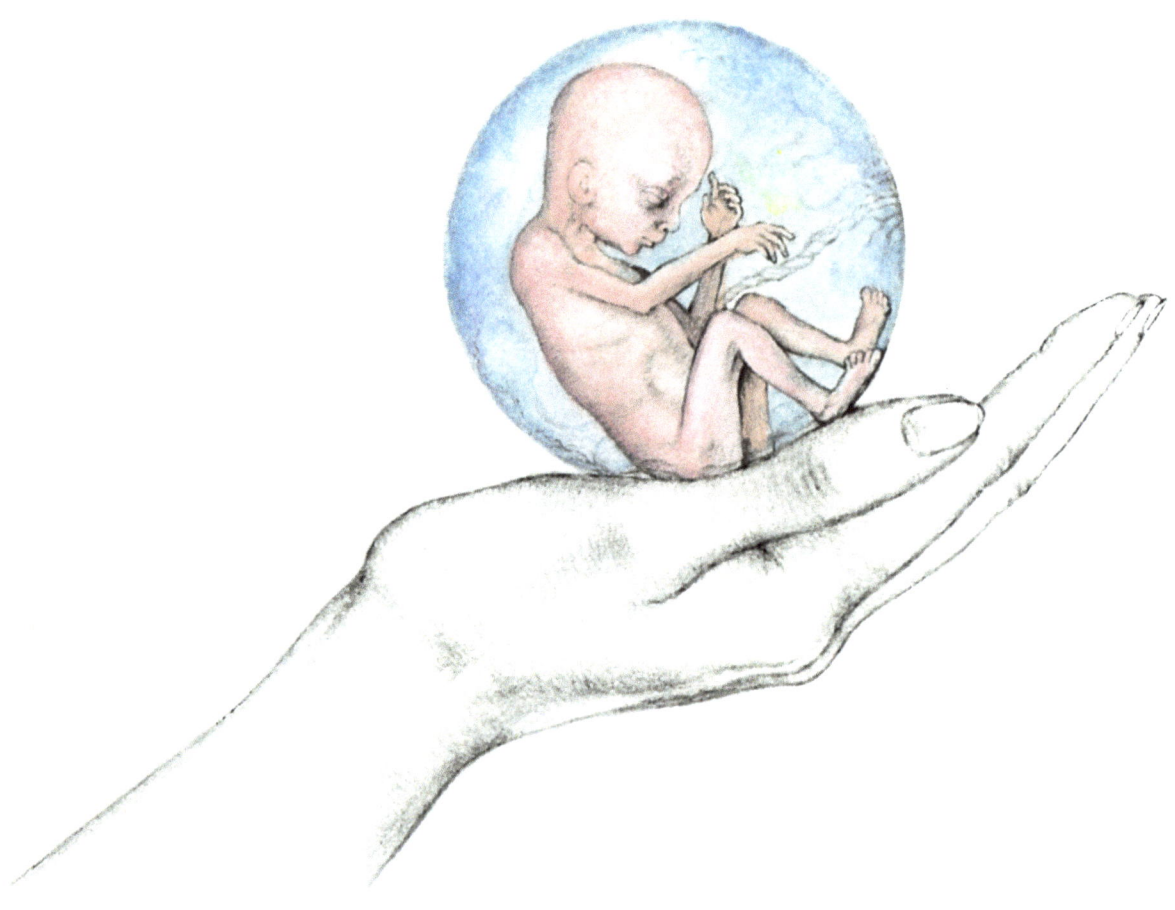

...to preach the acceptable year of the Lord.
Luke 4:18,19

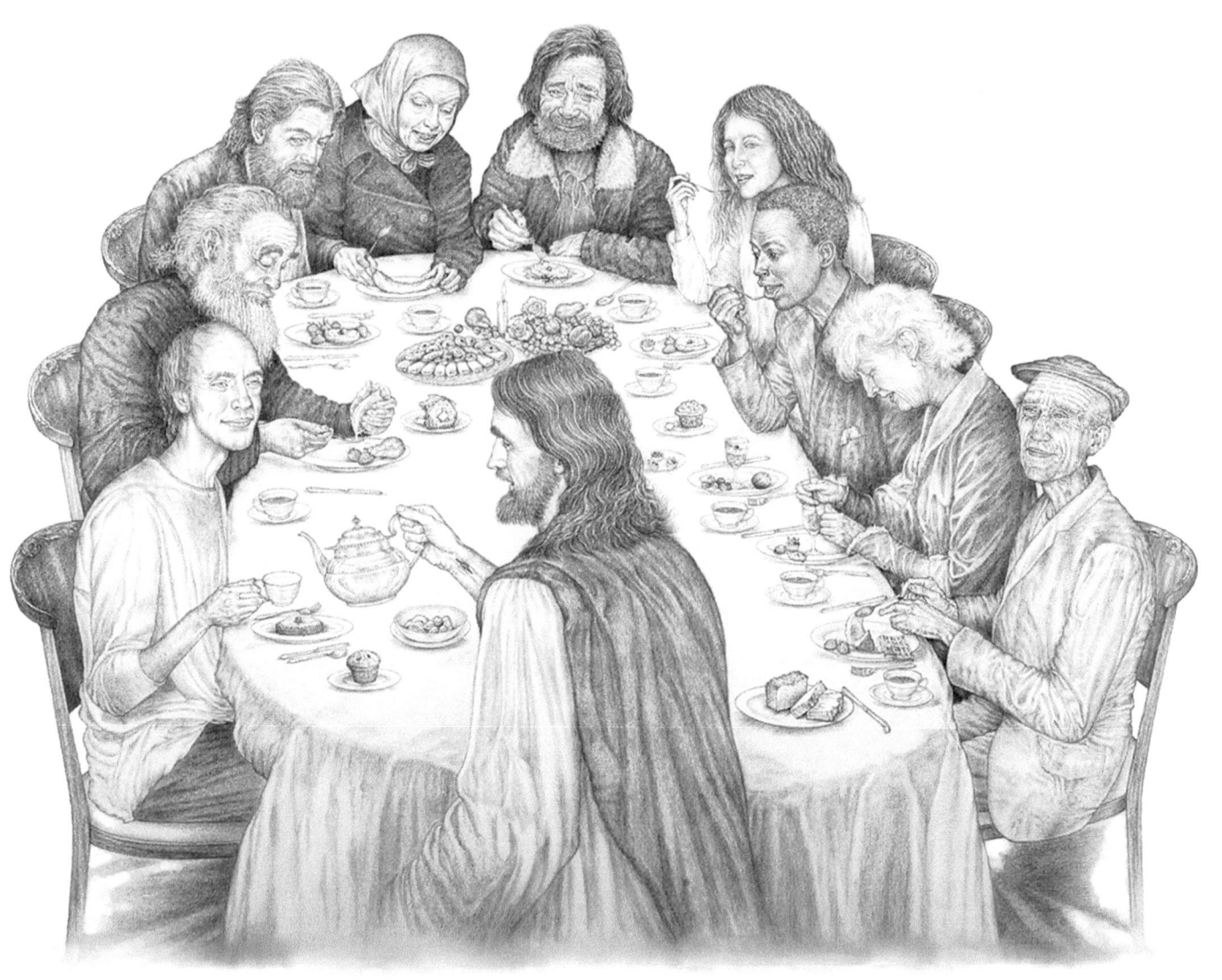

*When the Son of man shall come in His glory,
and all the holy angels with Him, then He shall sit upon the throne
of His glory: and before Him shall be gathered all nations: and He
shall separate them one from another, as a shepherd divides his
sheep from the goats: and He shall set the sheep on His right hand,
but the goats on the left. Then shall the King say to them on
His right hand,*

"Come, you blessed of My Father,
inherit the kingdom prepared
for you from
the foundation
of the world:

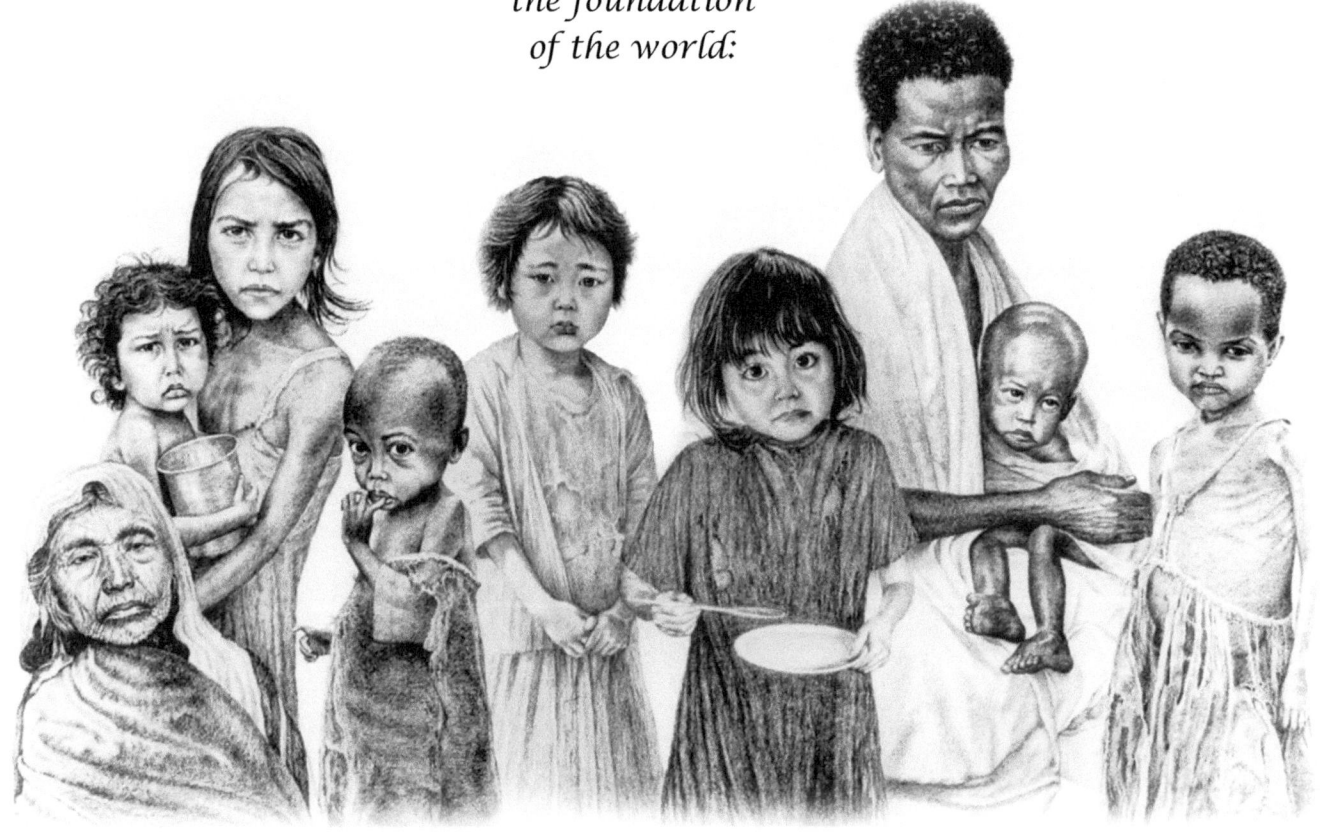

For I was hungry, and you gave Me food: I was thirsty, and you gave Me drink: I was a stranger, and you took Me in: naked, and you clothed Me: I was sick, and you visited me: I was in prison, and you came to Me."

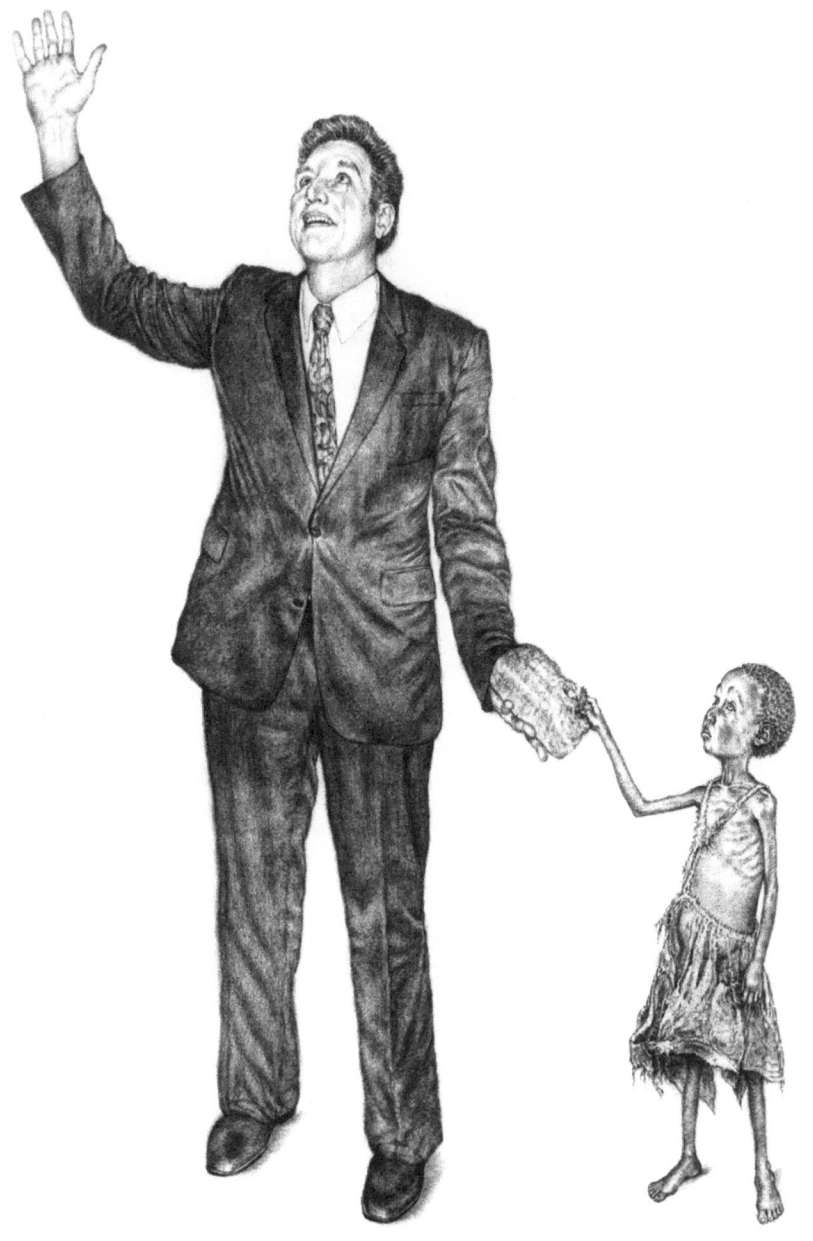

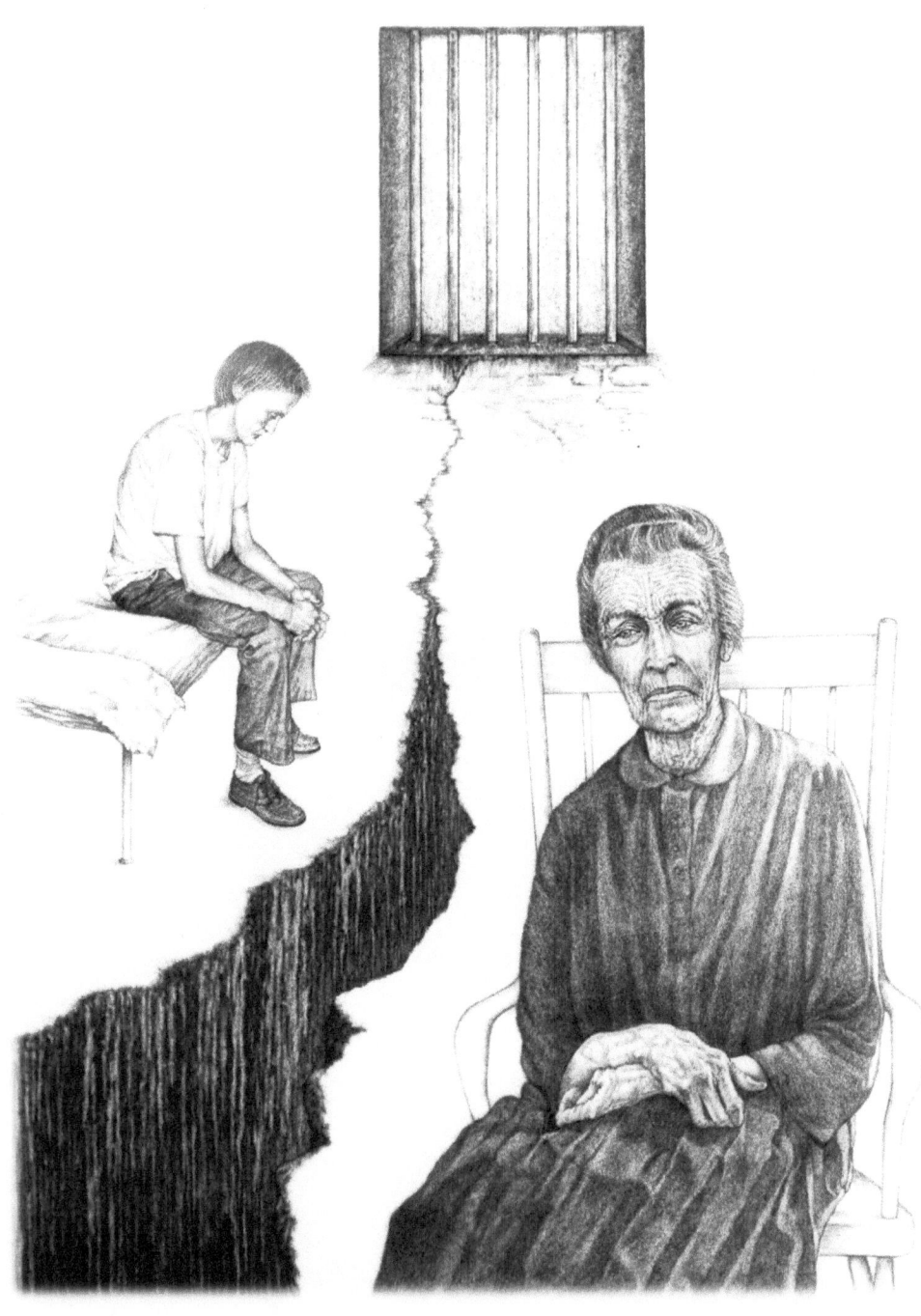

Then shall the righteous answer Him, saying, "Lord, when did we see You hungry, and fed You? or thirsty, and gave You drink? When did we see You a stranger, and took You in? or naked, and clothed You? Or when did we see You sick, or in prison, and came to You?"

And the King shall answer and say to them, "Truly I say to you, inasmuch as you have done it to one of the least of these My brethren, you have done it to Me." Matthew 25:31-40

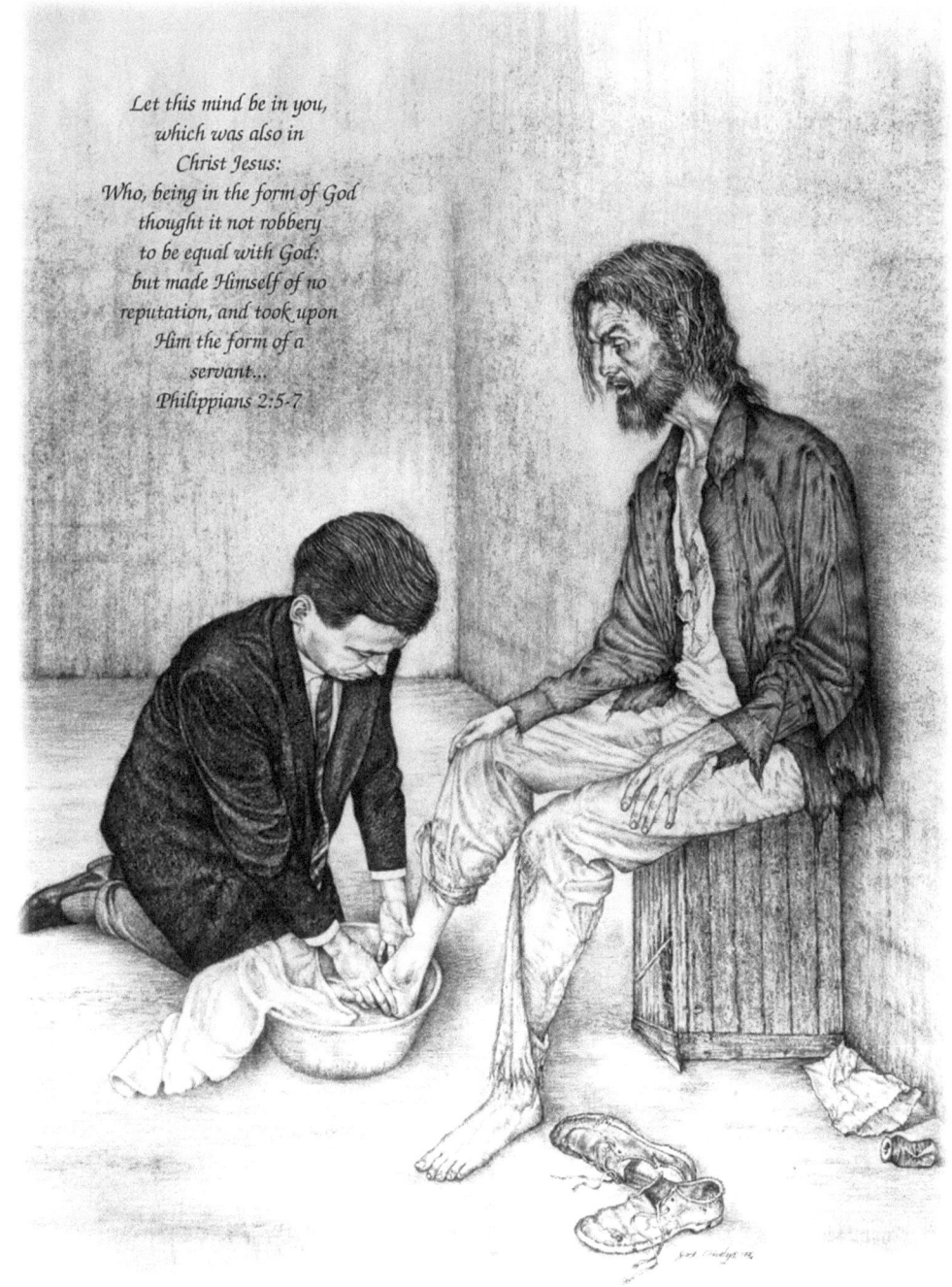

Let this mind be in you, which was also in Christ Jesus: Who, being in the form of God thought it not robbery to be equal with God: but made Himself of no reputation, and took upon Him the form of a servant...
Philippians 2:5-7

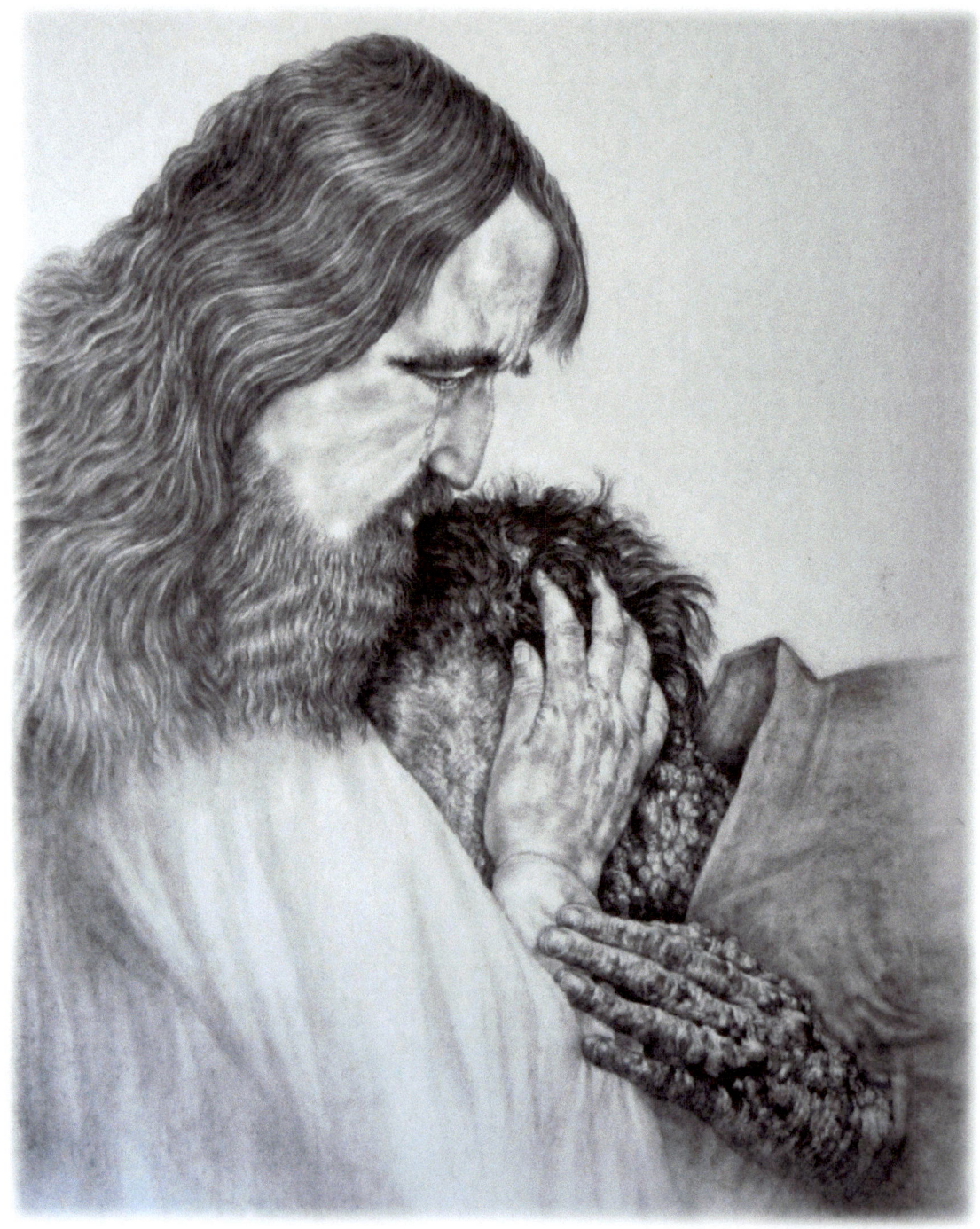

*For this
is the message
that you heard from the beginning,
that we should love one another.
I John 3:11*

*But whoever has
this world's good,
and sees his brother in need,
and shuts up his heart of compassion
from him, how dwells
the love of God in him?
My little children,
let us not love in word,
neither in tongue;
but in deed and in truth.
I John 3:17,18*

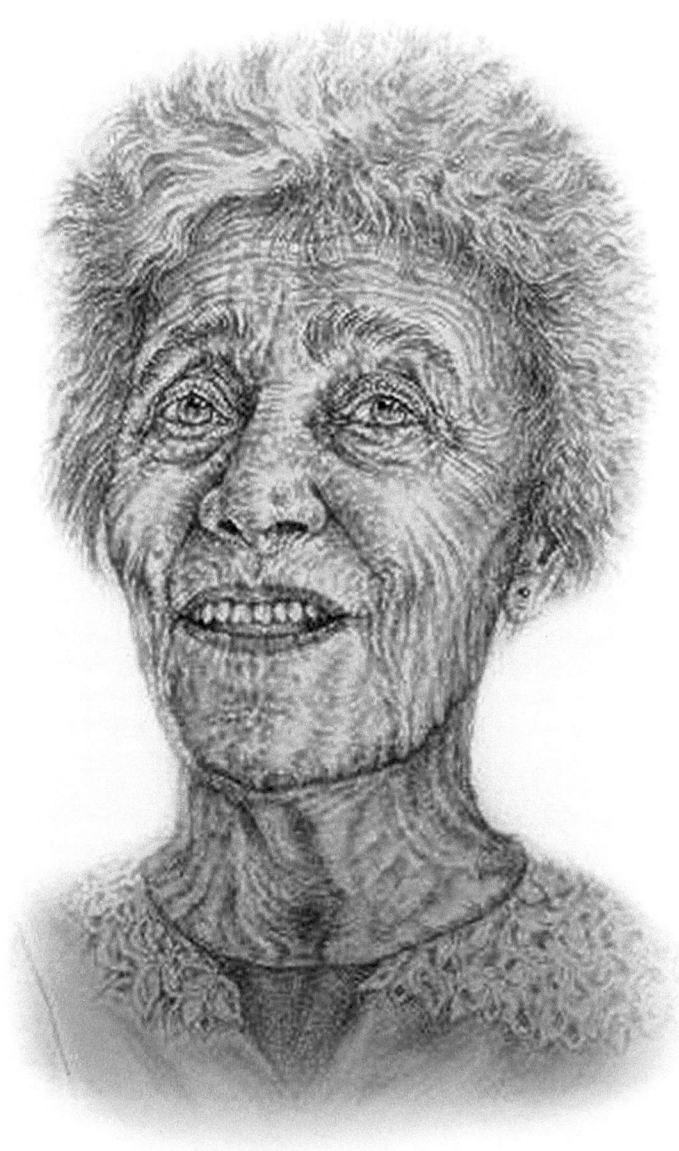

They shall still bring forth fruit in old age; they shall be fat and flourishing... Psalm 92:14

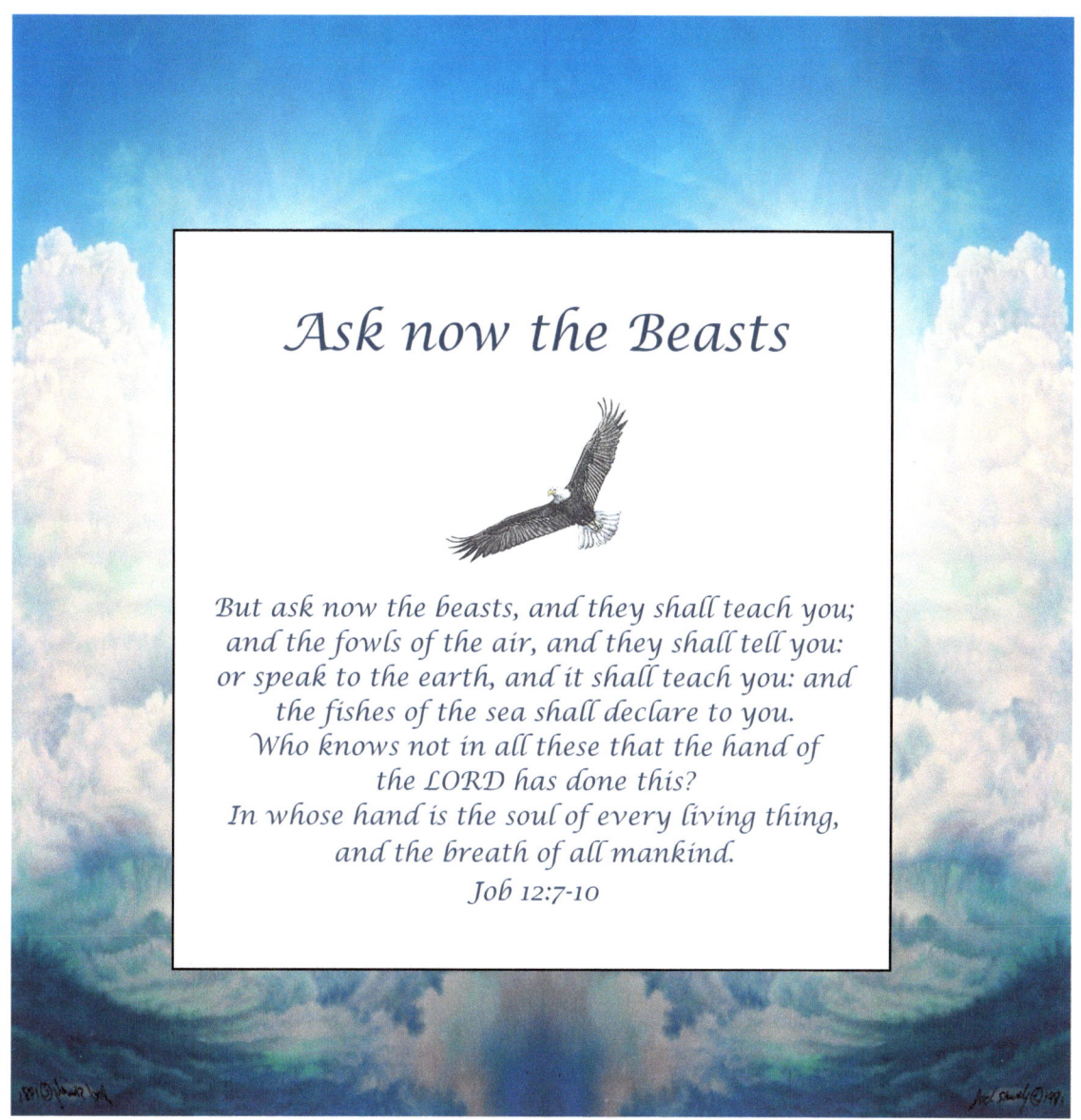

Ask now the Beasts

But ask now the beasts, and they shall teach you;
and the fowls of the air, and they shall tell you:
or speak to the earth, and it shall teach you: and
the fishes of the sea shall declare to you.
Who knows not in all these that the hand of
the LORD has done this?
In whose hand is the soul of every living thing,
and the breath of all mankind.
Job 12:7-10

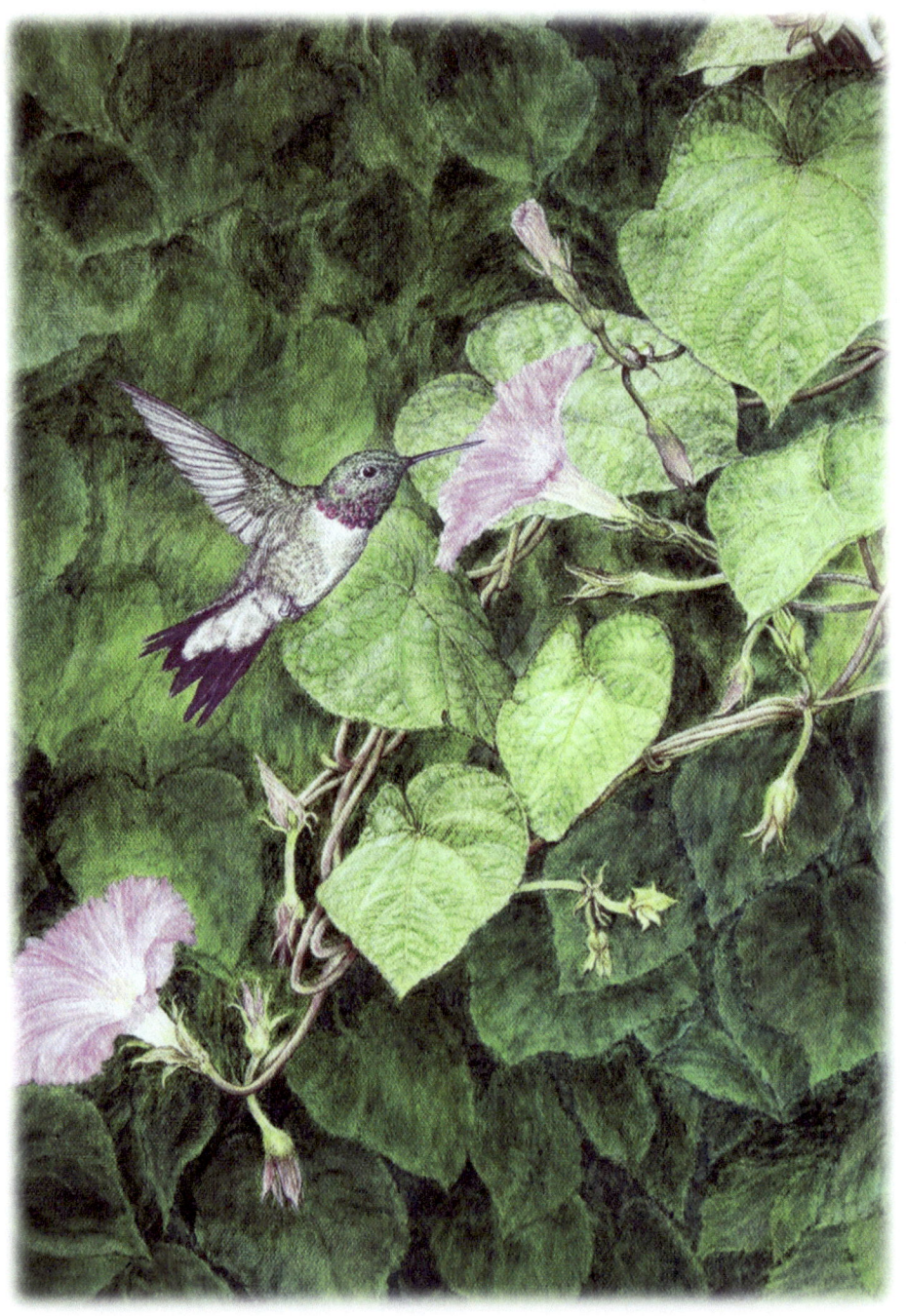

*Your words
were found and
I did eat them;
and Your word
was to me
the joy
and rejoicing
of my heart...
How sweet are Your
words to my taste!
Yes, sweeter than
honey
to my mouth!
Oh, taste and see
that the
LORD is good:
blessed
is the man who
trusts in Him.*

*Jeremiah 15:16,
Psalm 119:103,
Psalm 34:8*

*He that
has ears to
hear,
let him hear.
Matthew 11:15*

*Be still,
and know that
I am God:
I will be
exalted
among the
nations,
I will be
exalted
in the earth.
Psalm 46:10*

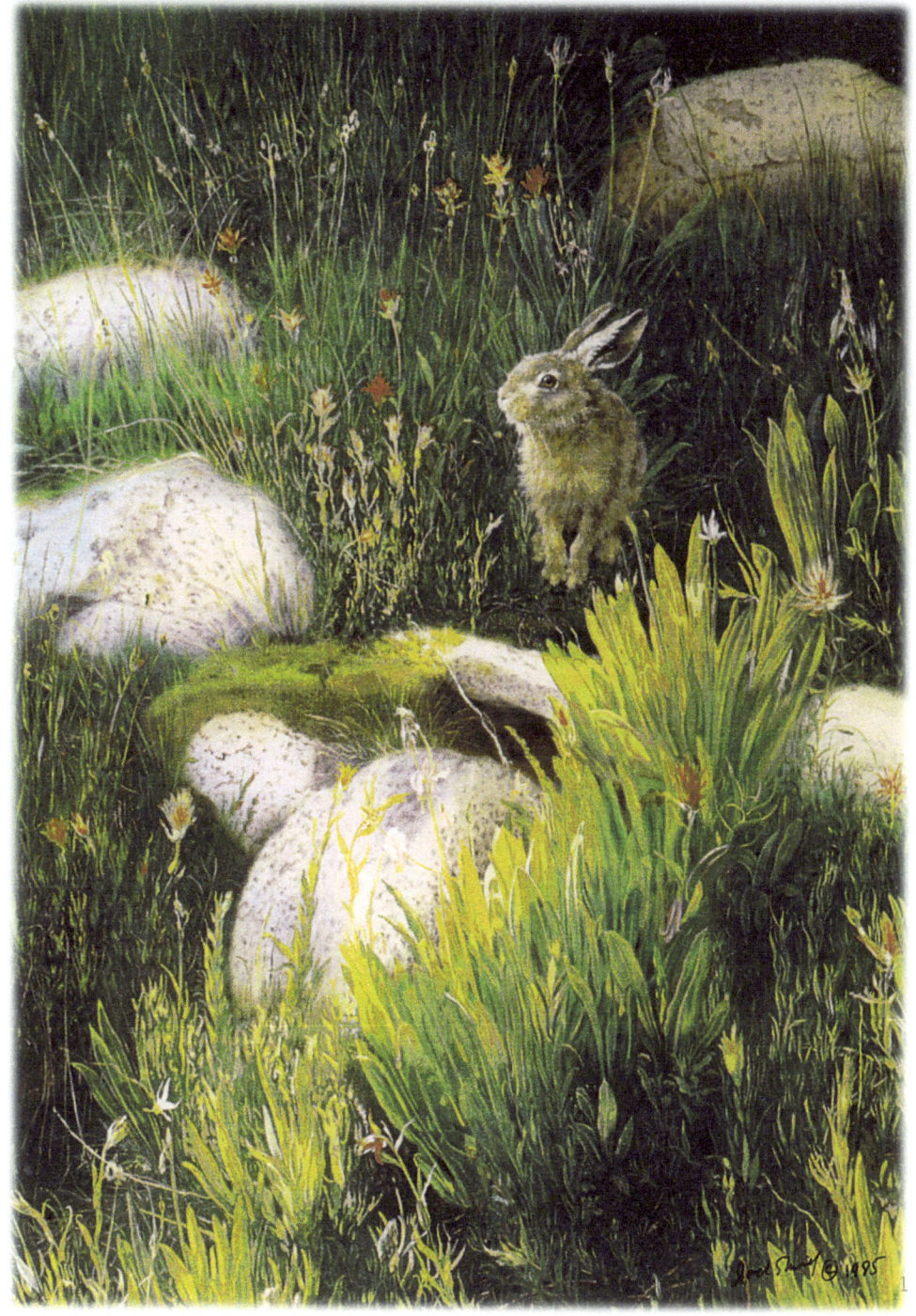

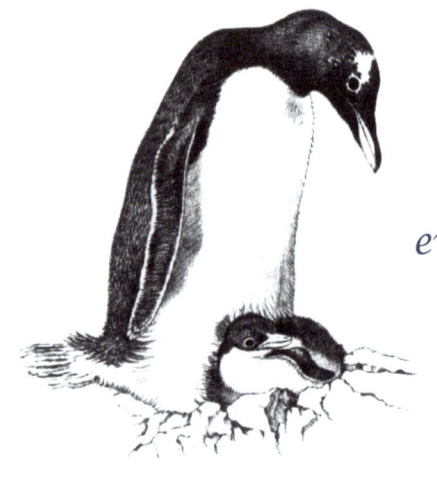

*As one whom his mother comforts,
so will I comfort you...
...I have made, and I will bear;
even I will carry, and I will deliver you.
Isaiah 66:13, 46:4*

*Blessed are the meek: for they shall
inherit the earth.
Matthew 5:5*

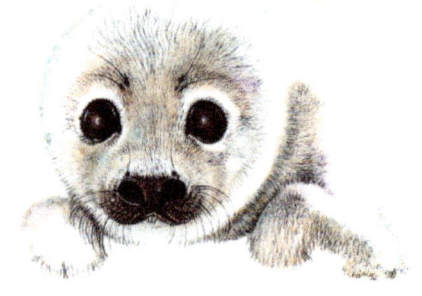

Love one another

*Behold, how good and how
pleasant it is for brethren to
dwell together in unity!
John 15:17, Psalm 133:1*

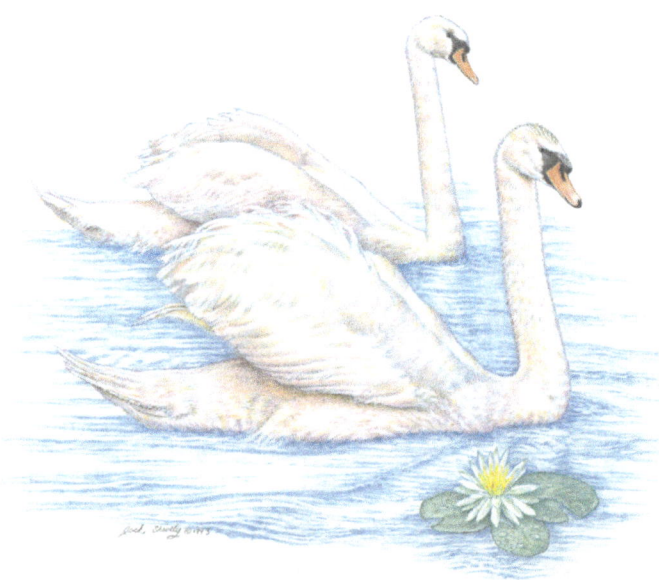

And you be kind to one another, tenderhearted, forgiving one another, even as God for Christ's sake has forgiven you.
Ephesians 4:32

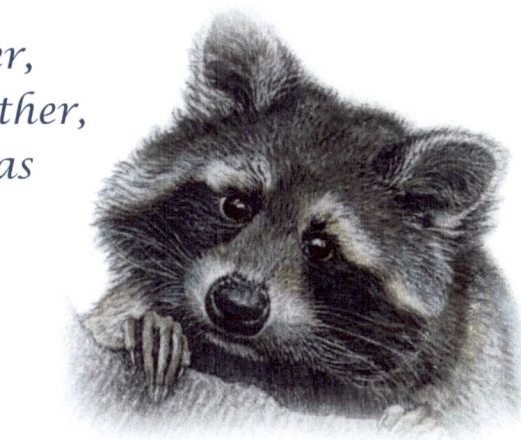

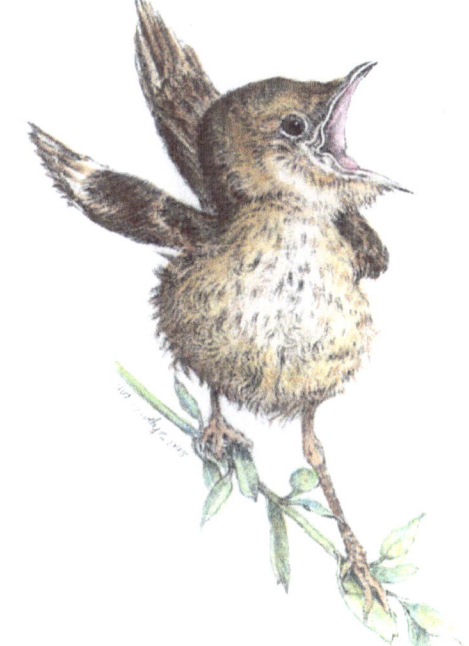

Let everything that has breath praise the LORD. Praise ye the LORD.
Psalm 150:6

When you lie down, you shall not be afraid: yes, you shall lie down, and your sleep shall be sweet. - Proverbs 3:24

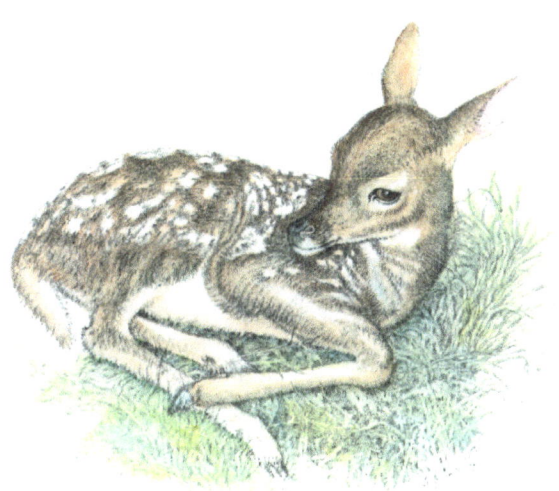

*They that wait upon the Lord
shall renew their strength; they shall mount
up with wings as eagles; they shall run,
and not be weary; and they shall
walk, and not faint.
Isaiah 40:31*

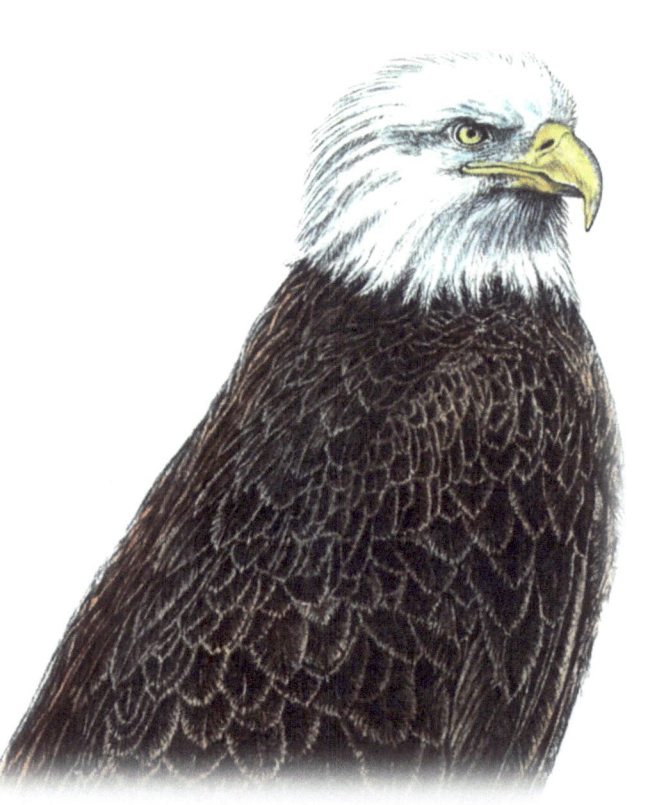

*Truly
my soul waits
upon God:
from Him comes
my salvation.
Psalm 62:1*

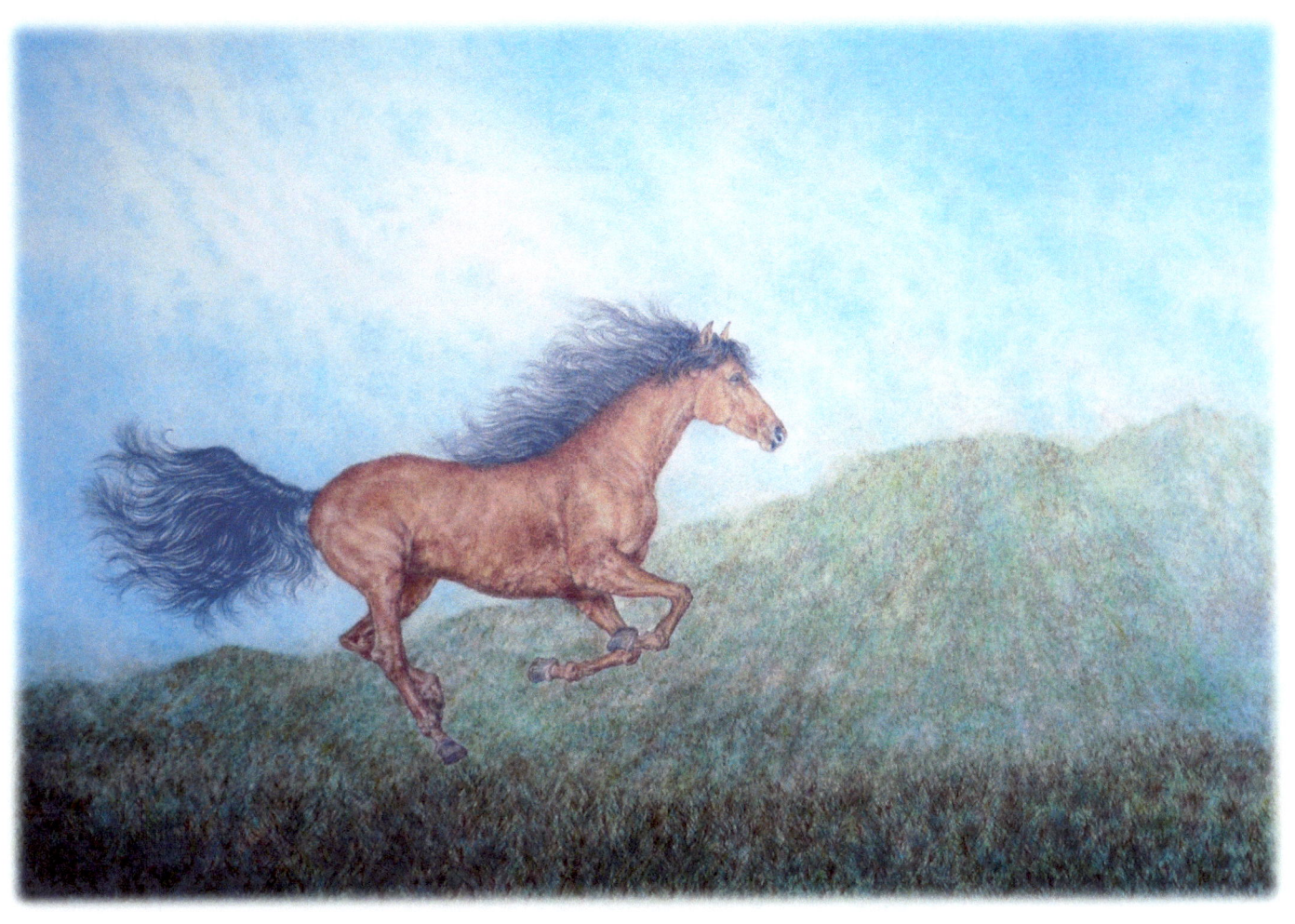

...And let us run with patience the race that is set before us, looking to Jesus the author and finisher of our faith... Hebrews 12:1,2

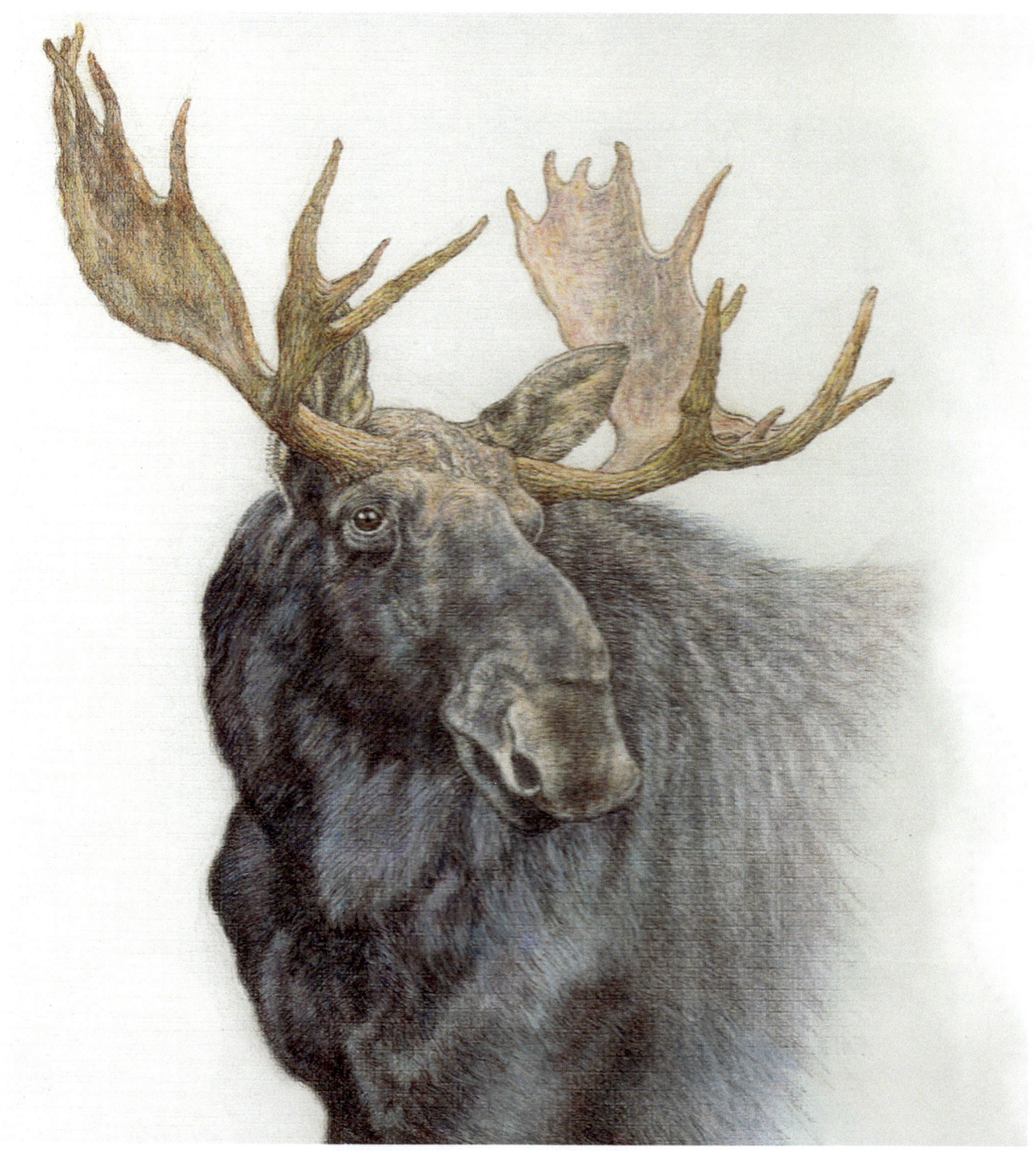

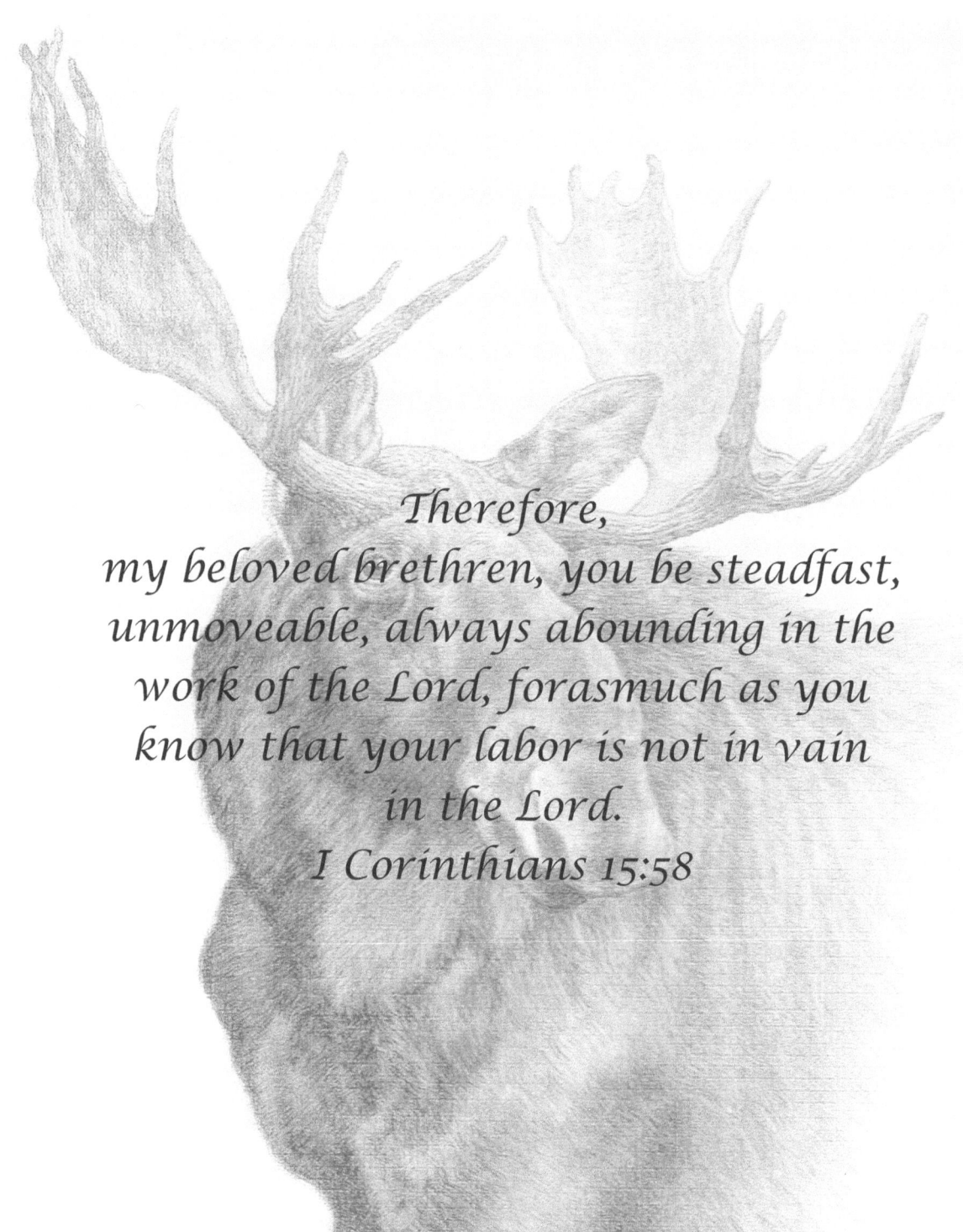

Therefore,
my beloved brethren, you be steadfast,
unmoveable, always abounding in the
work of the Lord, forasmuch as you
know that your labor is not in vain
in the Lord.
I Corinthians 15:58

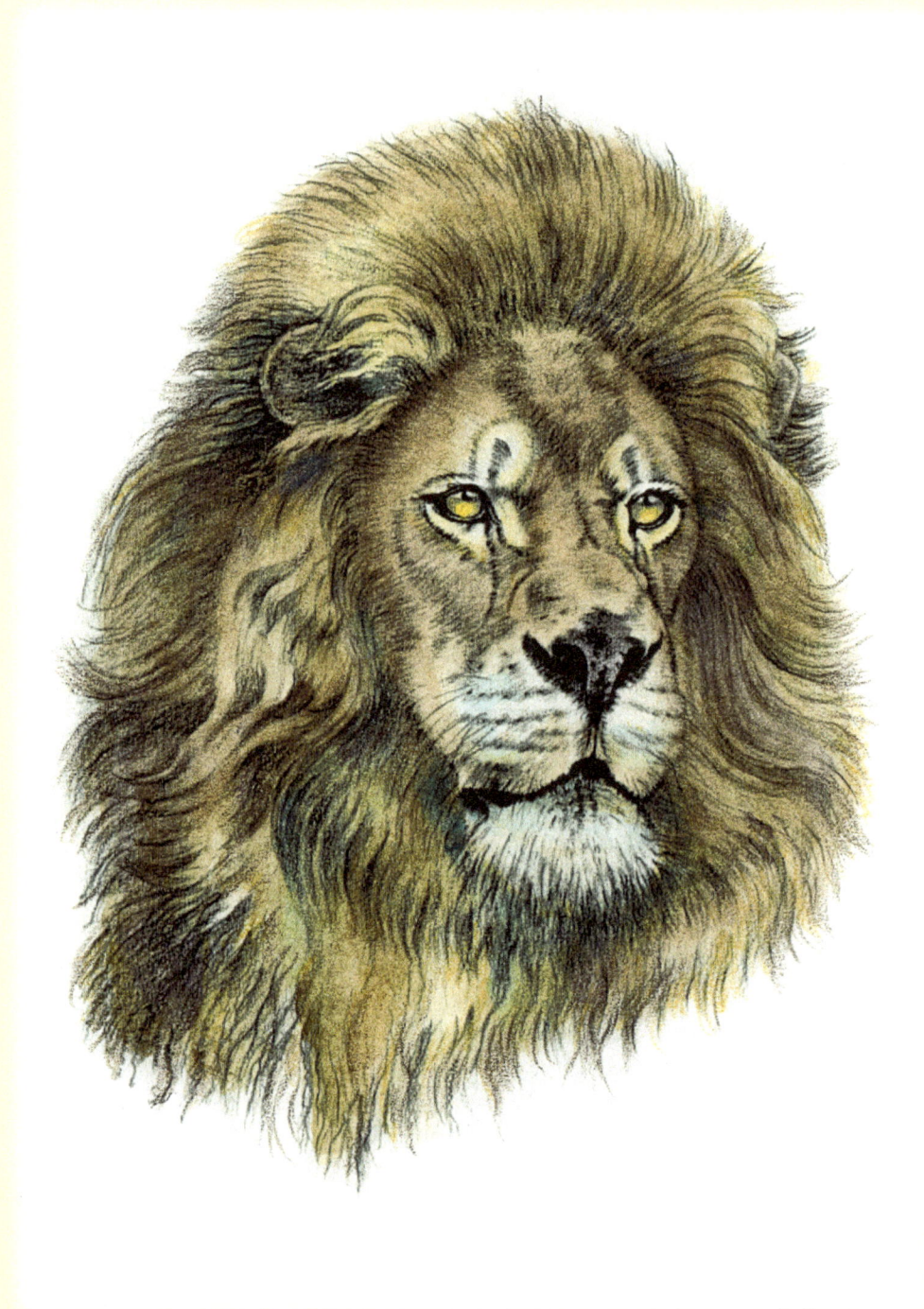

...Be Strong in the grace that is in Christ Jesus. - II Timothy 2:1

I can do
all things through
Christ who
strengthens me.
...You are strong, and the
word of God
abides in you, and you have
overcome the wicked one.
You are of God, little children,
and have overcome them:
because greater is He that is in you,
than he that is in the world.
Philippians 4:13,
I John 2:14, 4:4

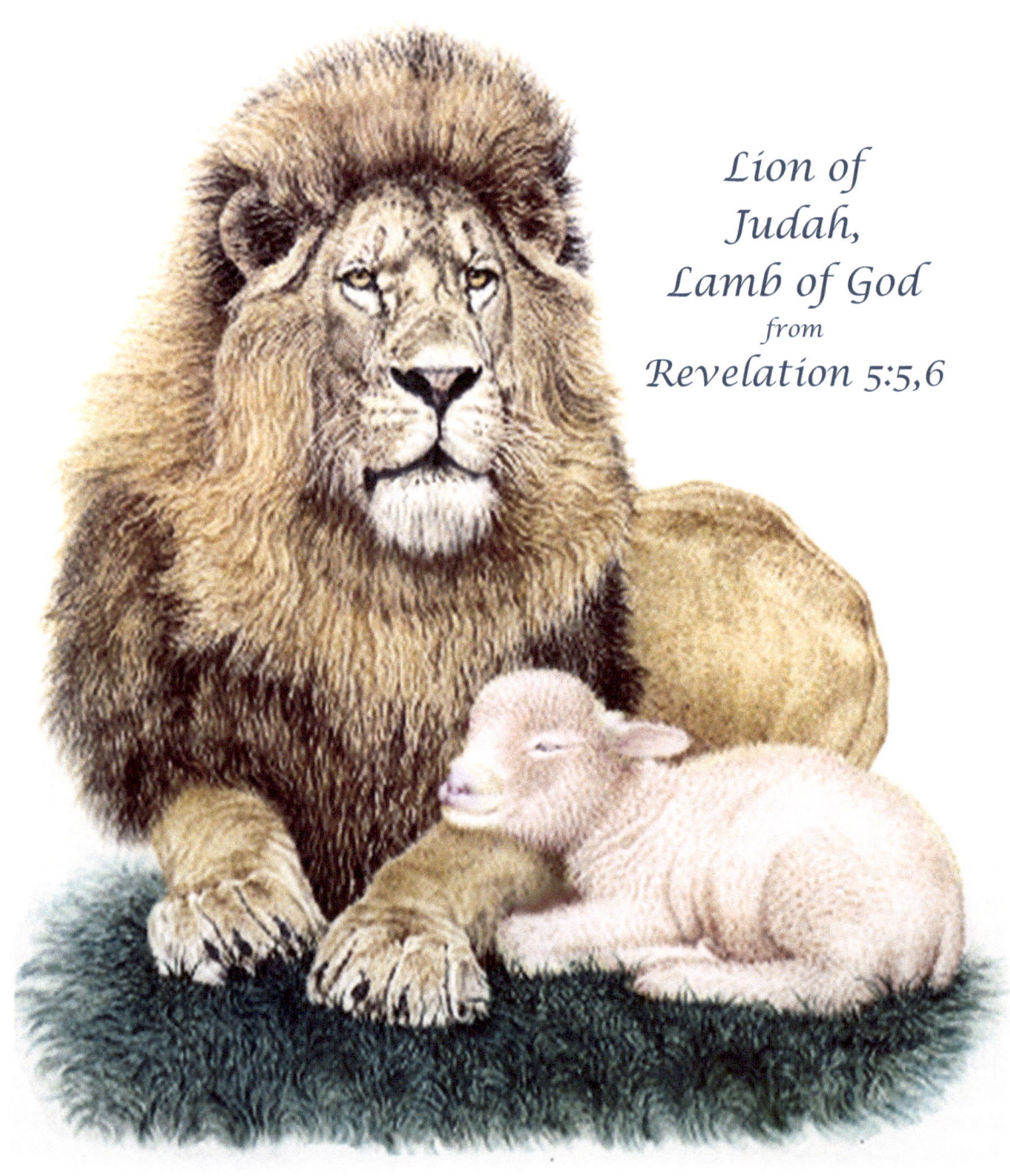

Lion of Judah, Lamb of God
from Revelation 5:5,6

...Behold the Lamb of God, who takes away the sin of the world. - John 1:29

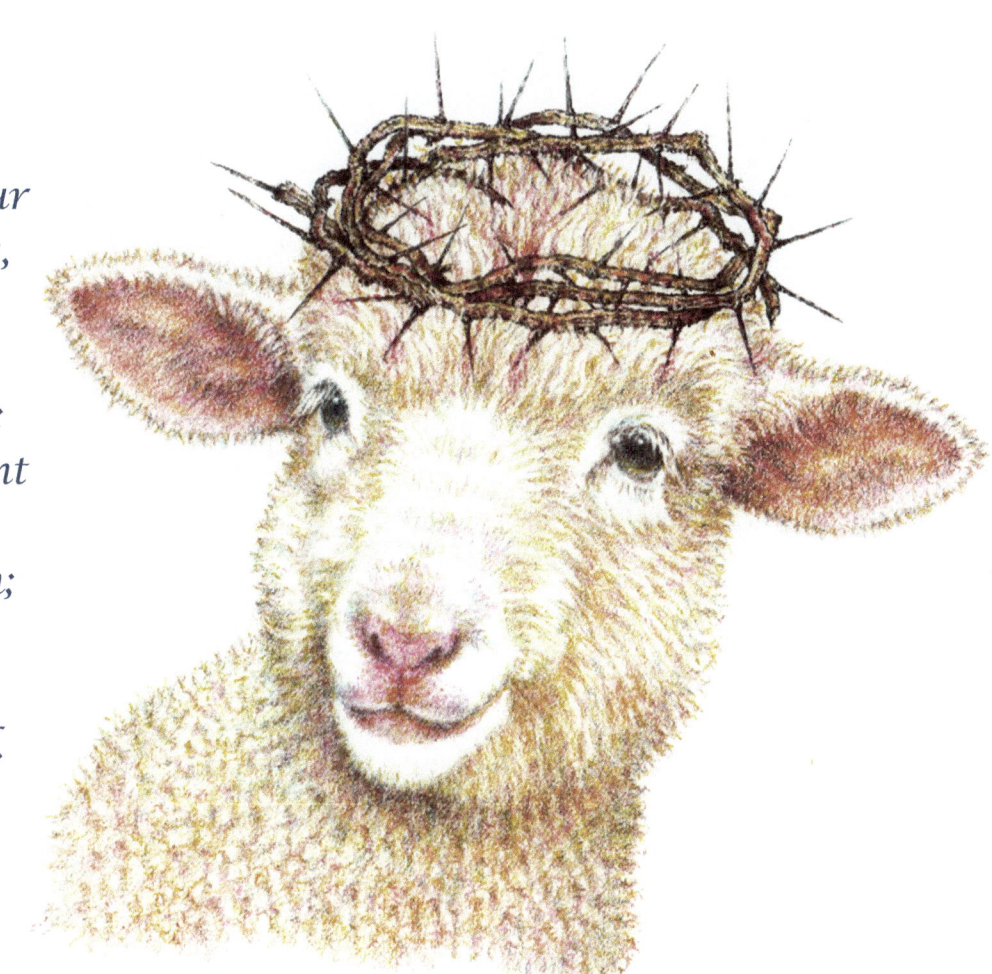

But He was wounded for our transgressions, He was bruised for our iniquities: the chastisement of our peace was upon Him; and with His stripes we are healed. Isaiah 53:5

*For God
so loved the world,
that He gave His only begotten Son, that
whoever believes in Him should not perish, but
have everlasting life.
John 3:16*

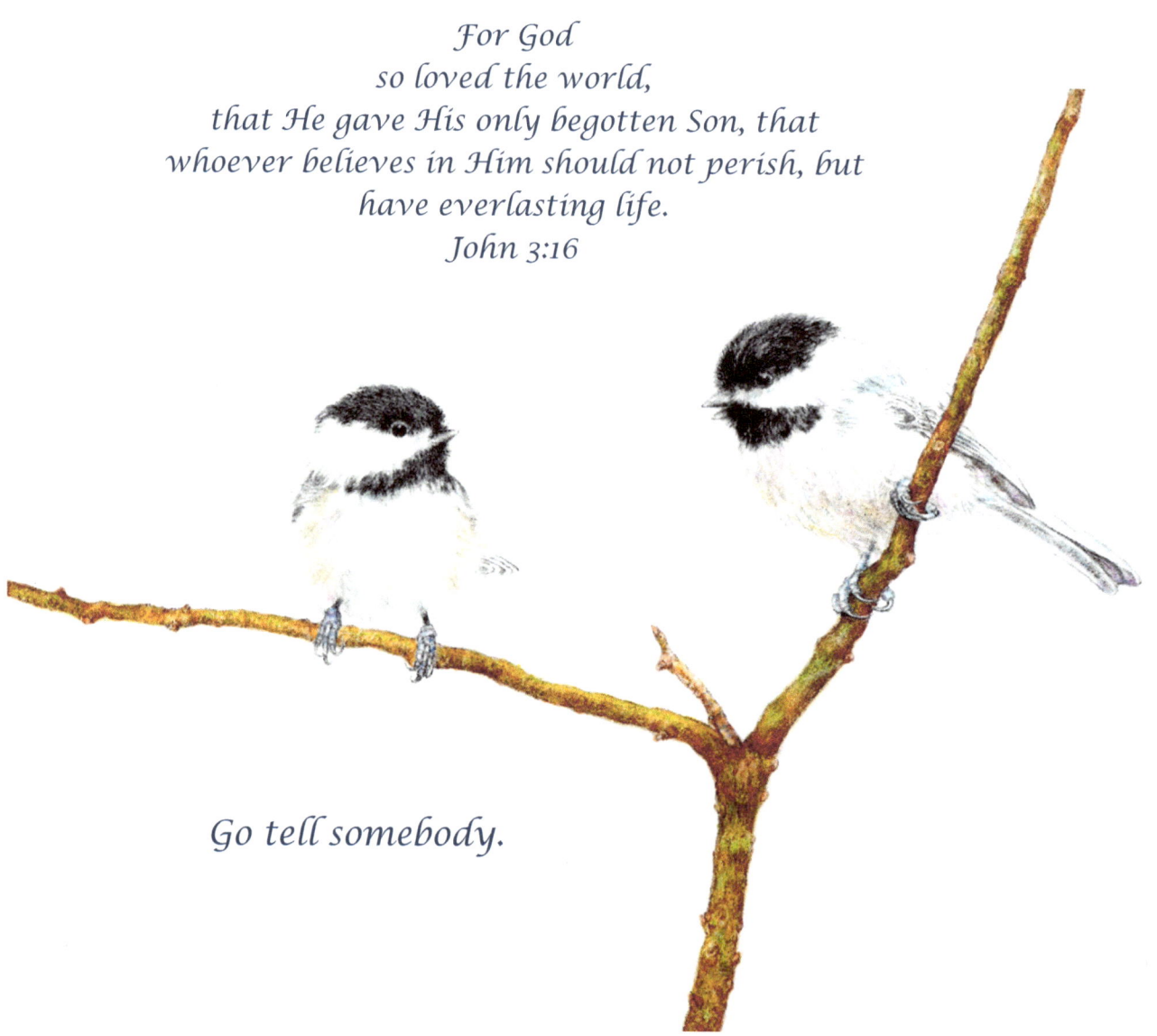

Go tell somebody.

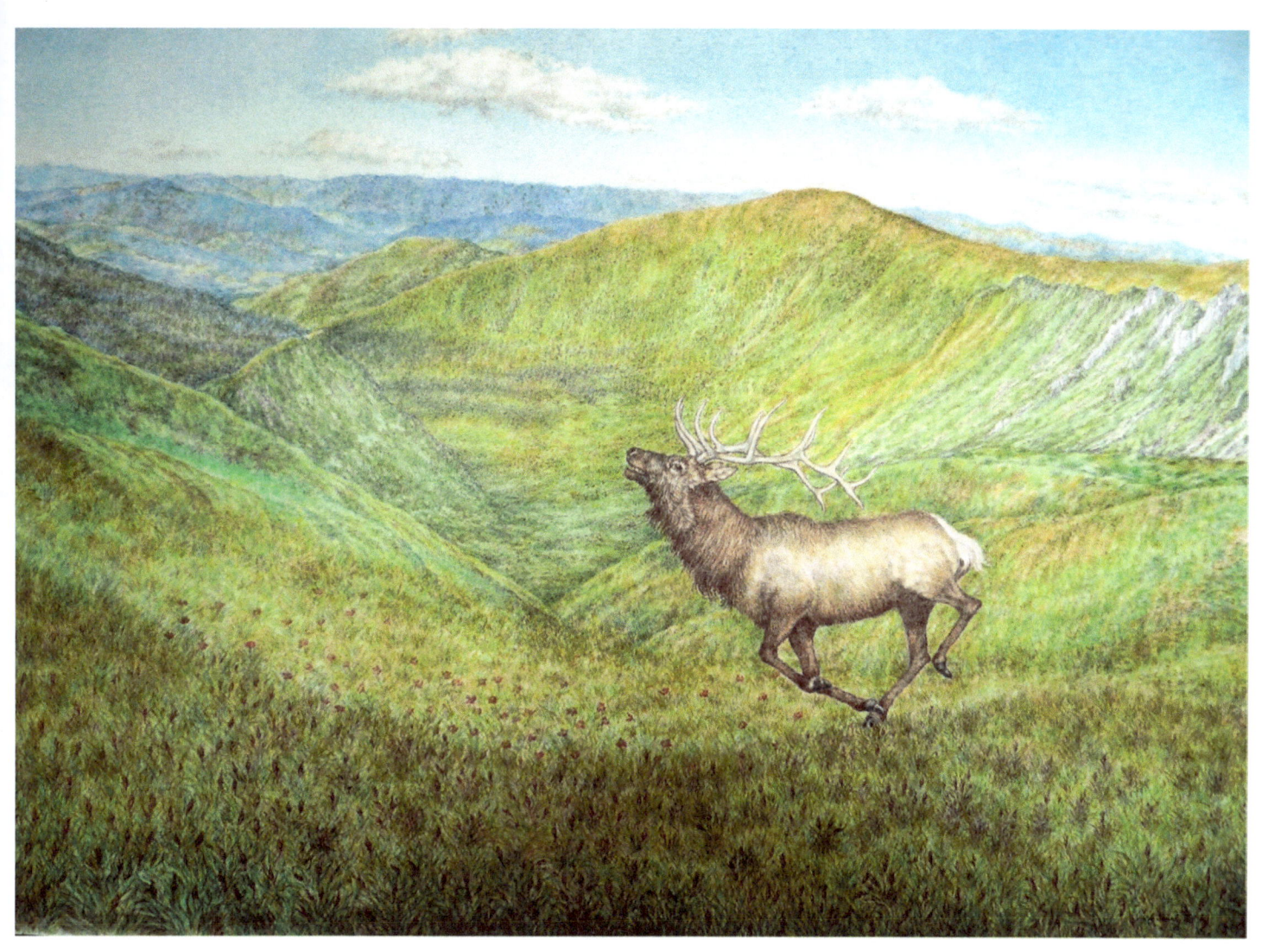

How beautiful upon the mountains are the feet of him that brings good tidings, that publishes peace; that brings good tidings of good, that publishes salvation; that says to Zion, your God reigns! - Isaiah 52:7

*For here
we have no continuing city,
but we seek one to come.
Hebrews 13:14
For we know that if our earthly house
of this tabernacle were dissolved,
we have a building of God,
a house not made with hands,
eternal in the heavens.
II Corinthians 5:1
For our citizenship is in heaven;
from where also we look for the Savior,
the Lord Jesus Christ: For the Lord himself shall descend
Philippians 3:20 from heaven with a shout, with the
voice of the archangel, and with the
trumpet of God: and the dead in
Christ shall rise first:
then we who are alive and remain
shall be caught up together with
them in the clouds, to meet the Lord
in the air: and so shall we always be
with the Lord.
Therefore comfort one another
with these words.
I Thessalonians 4:16-18*

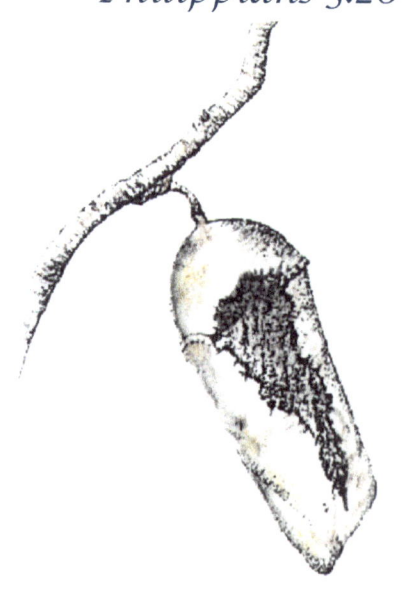

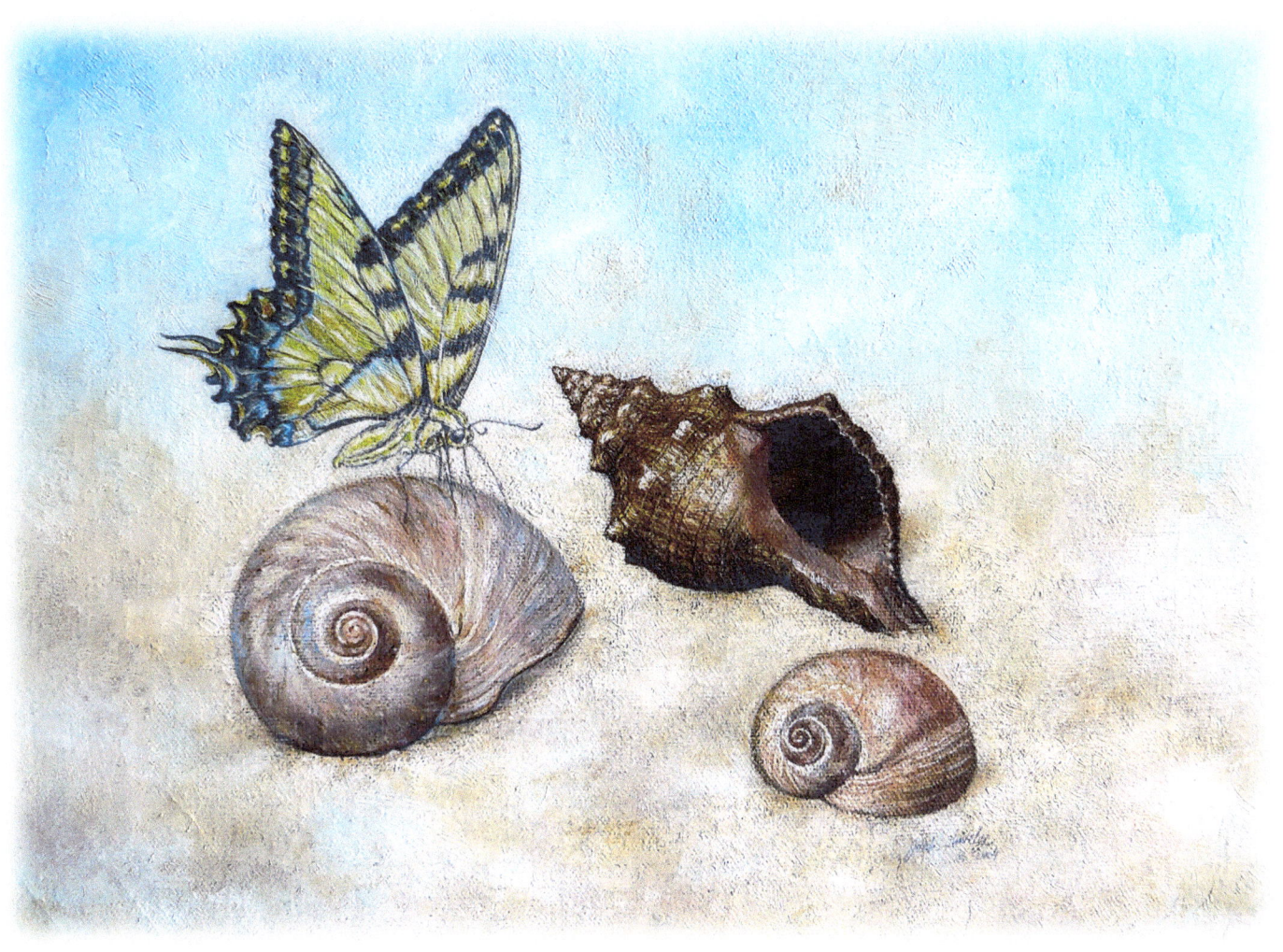

*Set your affection on things above,
not on things on the earth.
Colossians 3:2*

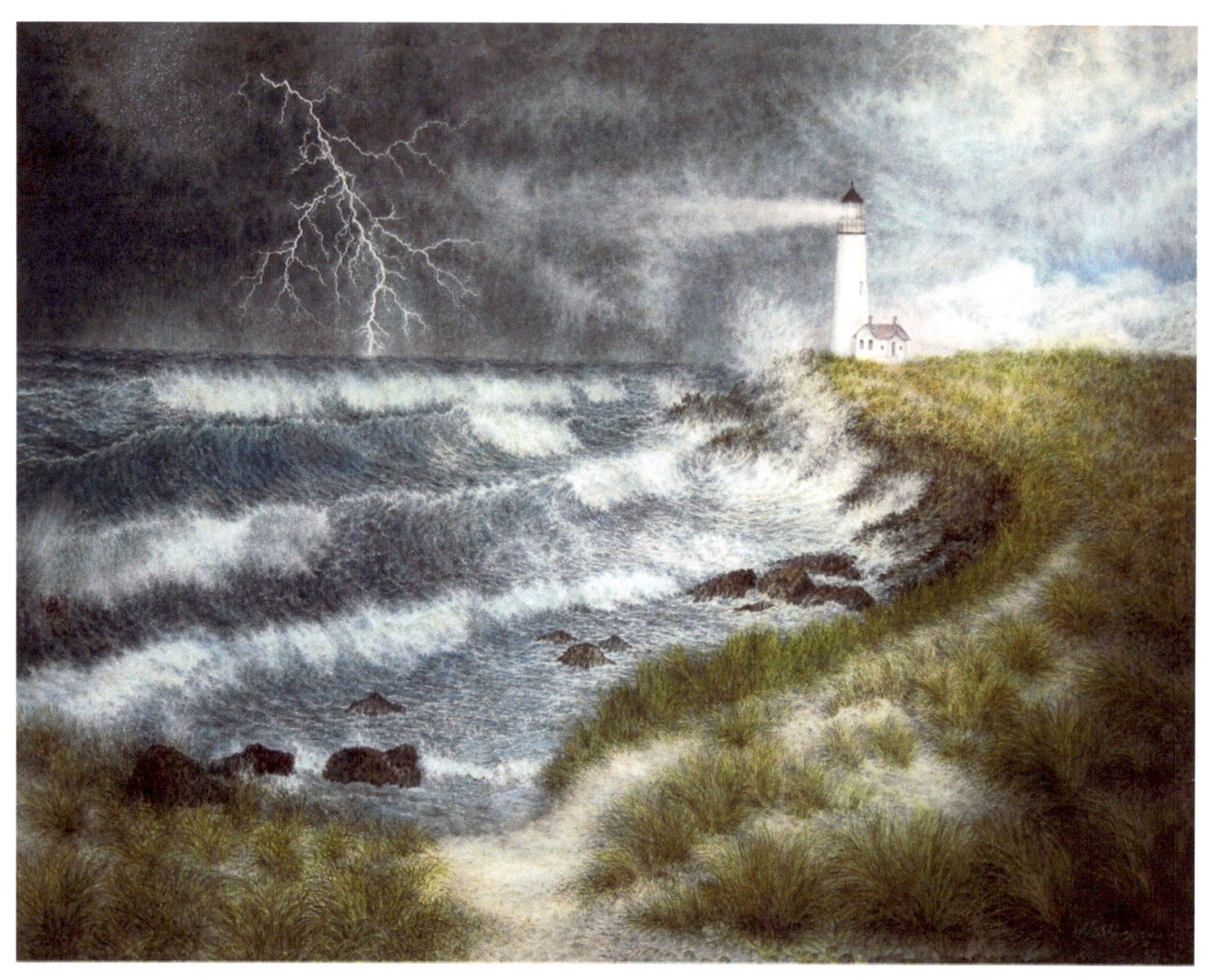

*The name of the LORD is a strong tower:
the righteous run into it, and are safe.*
Proverbs 18:10

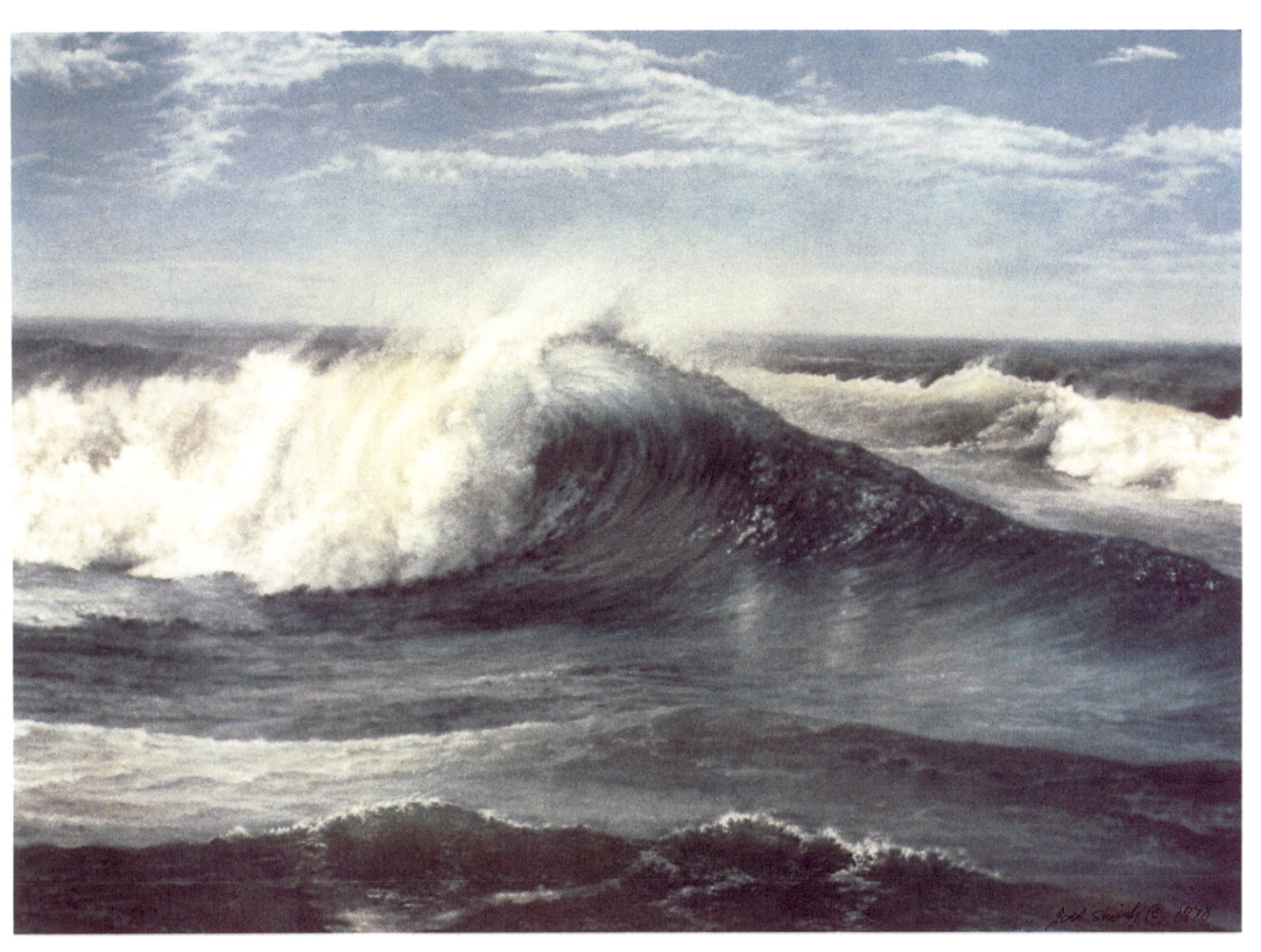

*You rule the raging of the sea: when the waves
thereof arise You still them.*
Psalm 89:9

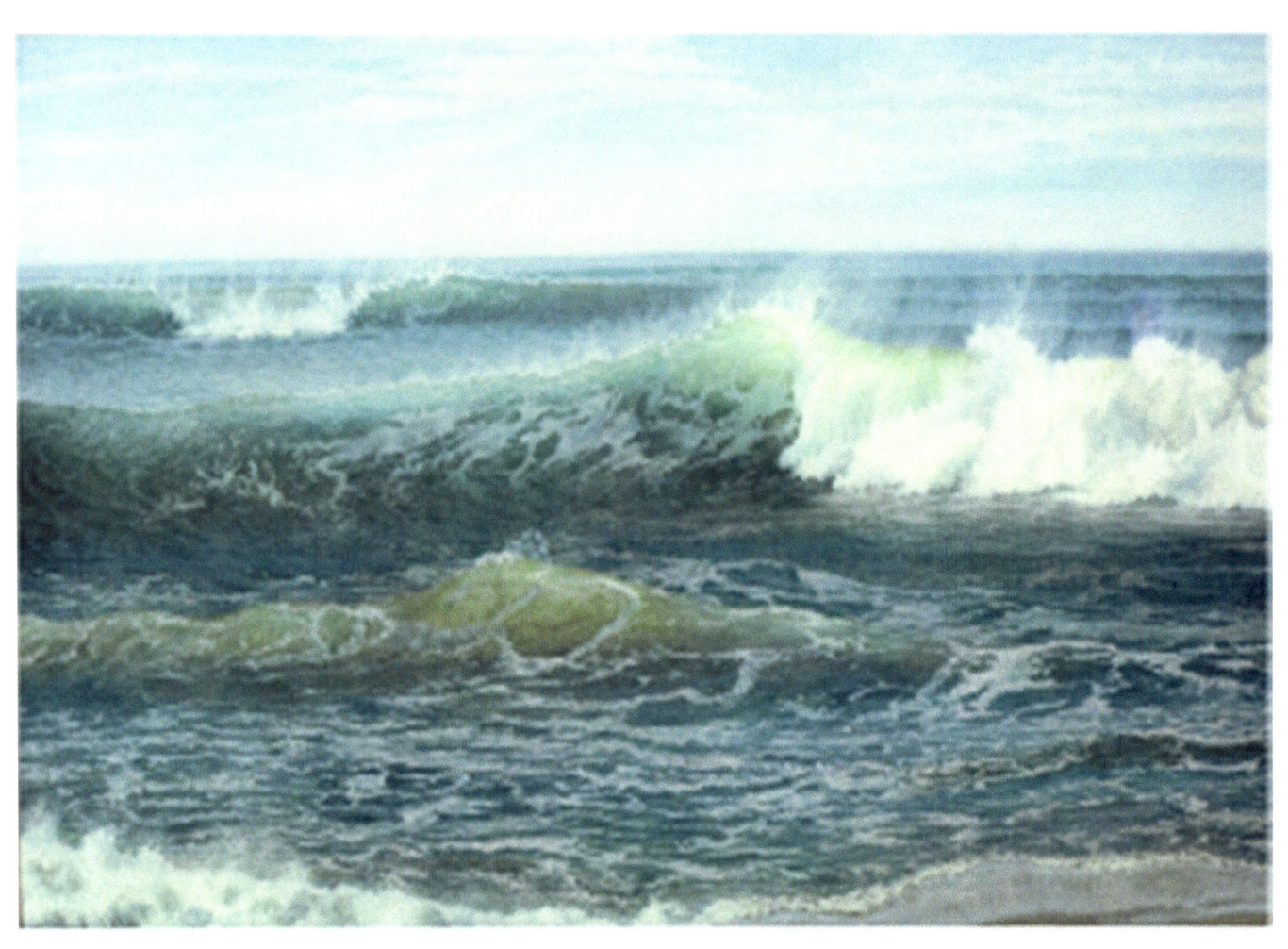

The voice of the LORD is upon the waters: the God of glory thunders: the LORD is upon many waters.
Psalm 29:3

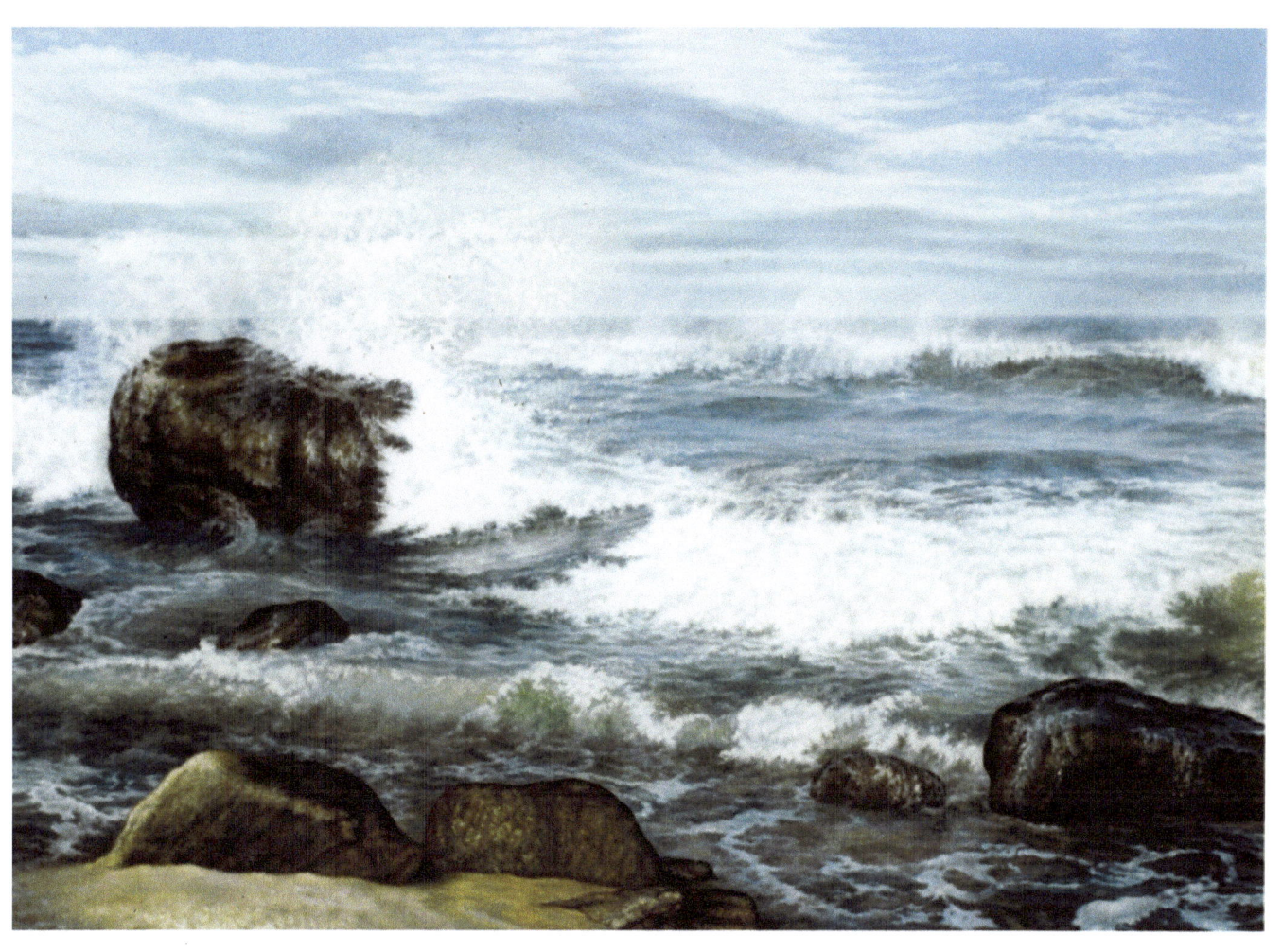

...When the enemy shall come in like a flood,
the Spirit of the LORD shall lift up a standard against him.
Isaiah 59:19

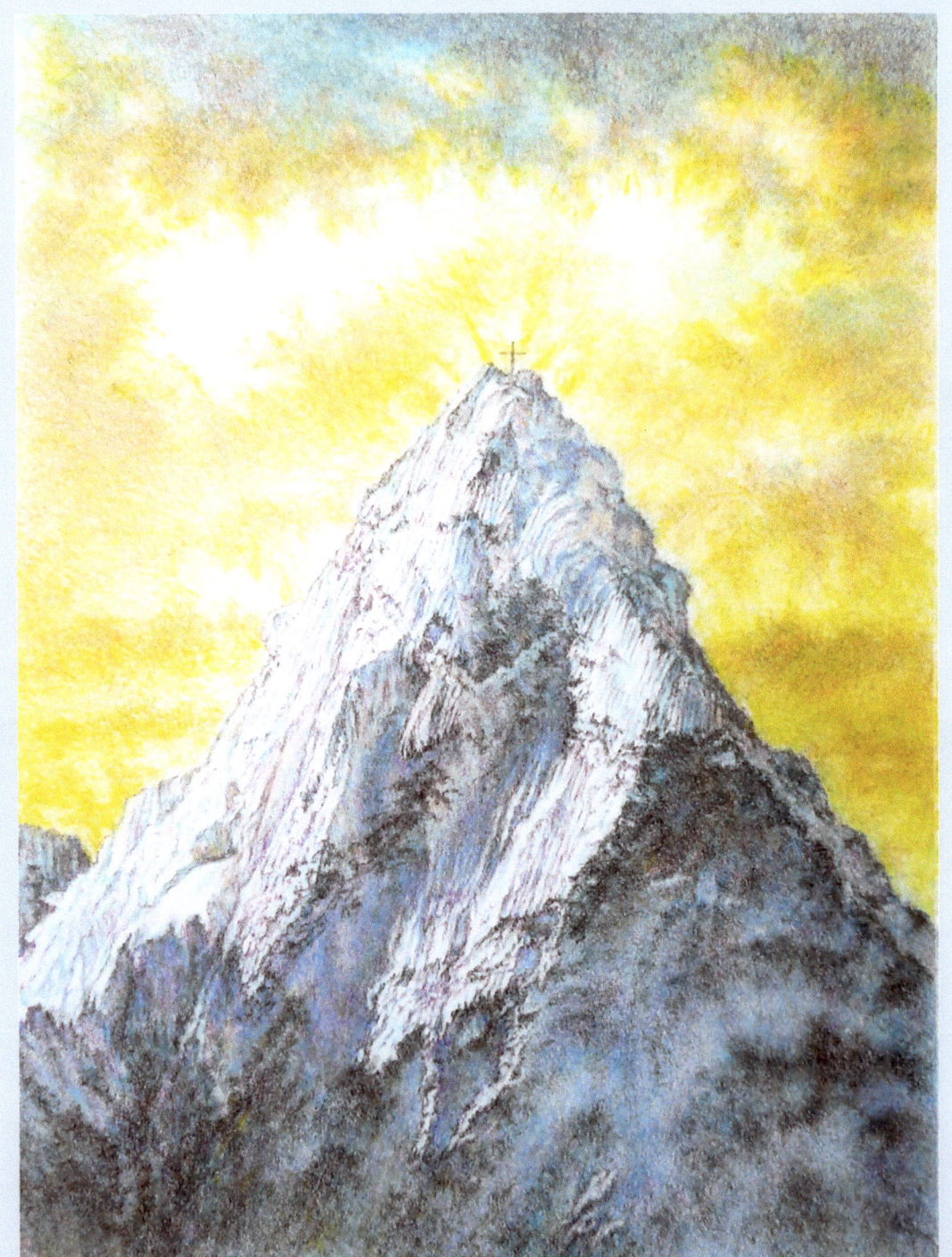

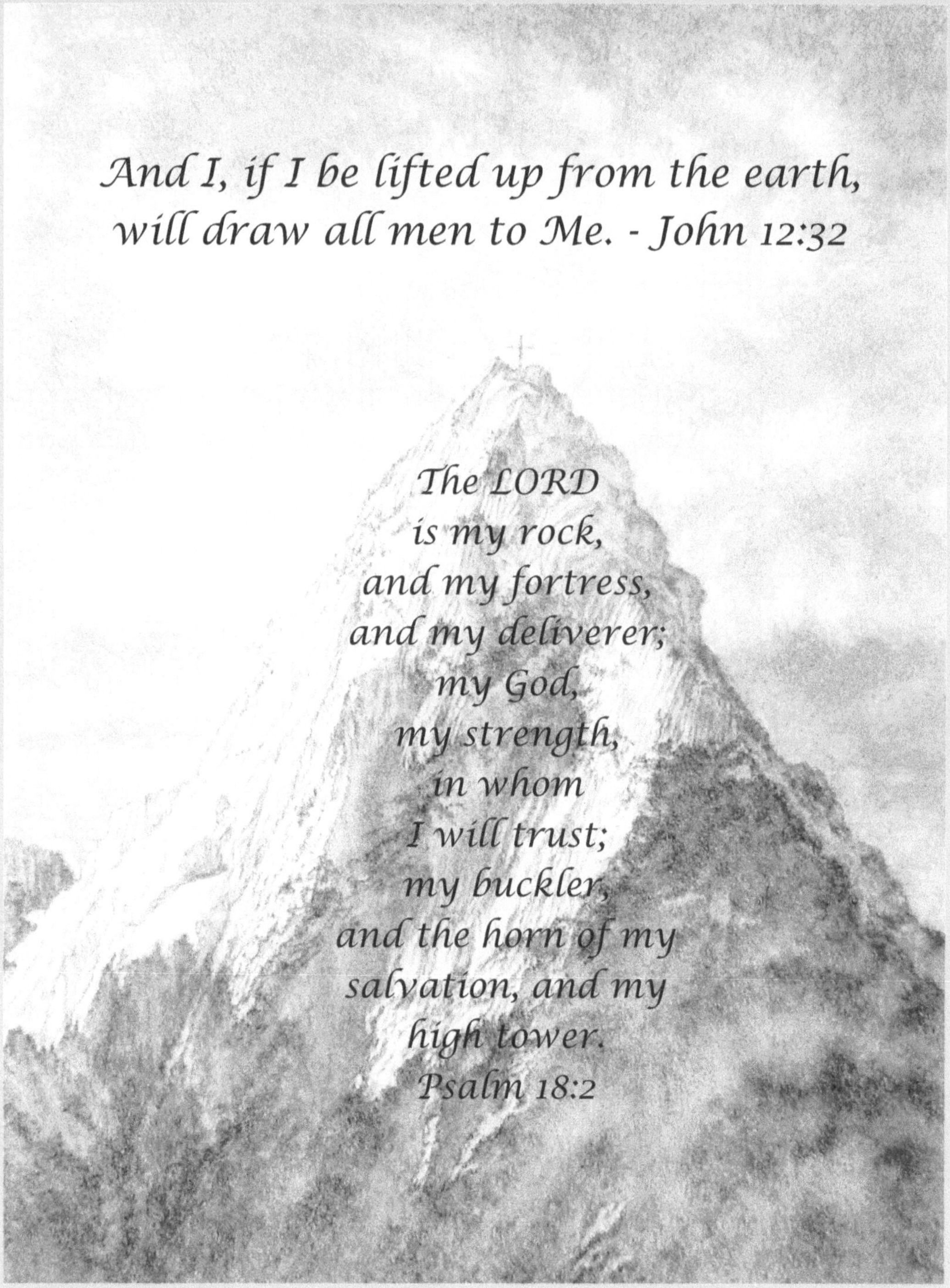

And I, if I be lifted up from the earth, will draw all men to Me. - John 12:32

*The LORD
is my rock,
and my fortress,
and my deliverer;
my God,
my strength,
in whom
I will trust;
my buckler,
and the horn of my
salvation, and my
high tower.
Psalm 18:2*

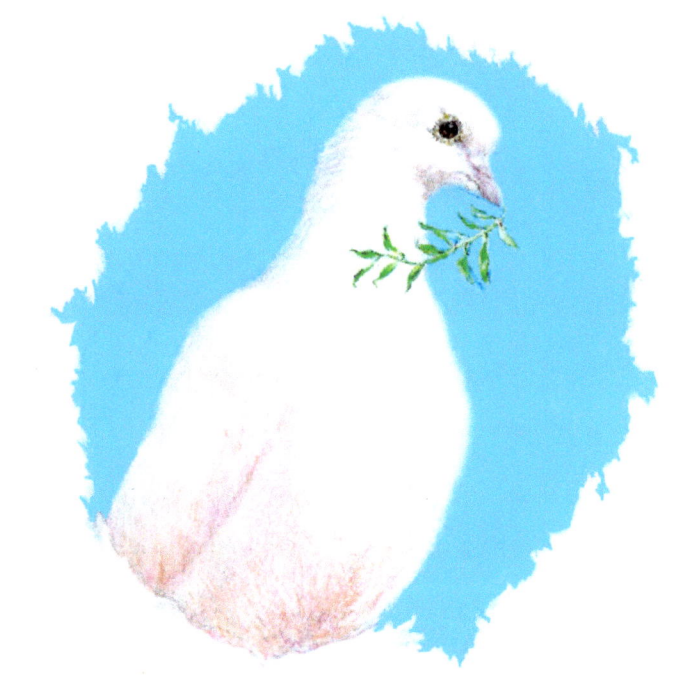

Peace be to you.
John 20:26